IMAGES
of America

LAKEWOOD
THEATRE COMPANY

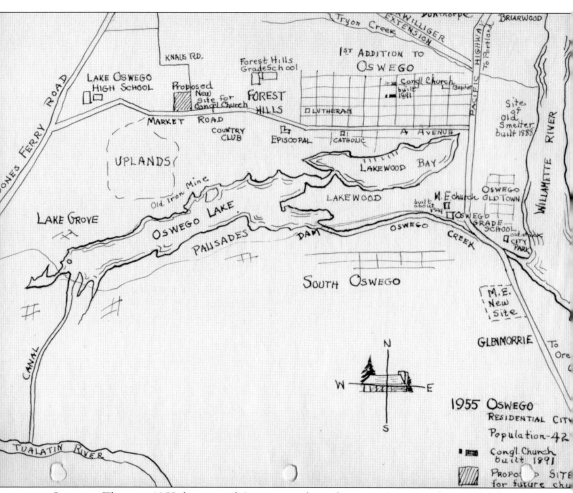

OSWEGO. This is a 1955 drawing of Oswego residential city in Oregon. The Town of Oswego was founded in 1847 by Albert Alonzo Durham, and he named the town after his birthplace in New York. With the annexation of part of Lake Grove to the west in 1960, the name of the city was changed to Lake Oswego. Oswego Grade School, renamed Lakewood Grade School in 1955 (and later known as Lakewood School), is located at 368 S. State Street; today, the building houses the Lakewood Center for the Arts. North of the Oswego Grade School building is the old Methodist Episcopal church (labeled "ME Church" in this drawing). (Courtesy of Lake Oswego Public Library and City of Lake Oswego.)

ON THE COVER: CABARET. In 1973, the cast of *Cabaret* took the stage. (Courtesy of Lakewood Theatre Company.)

IMAGES
of America
LAKEWOOD
THEATRE COMPANY

Jen Avila-Langford
Foreword by Kay Griffin Vega

ARCADIA
PUBLISHING

Published by Arcadia Publishing
Charleston, South Carolina

Printed in the United States of America

Library of Congress Control Number: 2021951088

For all general information, please contact Arcadia Publishing:
Telephone 843-853-2070
Fax 843-853-0044
E-mail sales@arcadiapublishing.com
For customer service and orders:
Toll-Free 1-888-313-2665

Visit us on the Internet at www.arcadiapublishing.com

*To my loving husband, Rob, and sons Kyle and Dylan.
To my mom and aunt, who inspire me every day.*

CONTENTS

FOREWORD

In 1972, I was invited to audition at Lake Oswego Community Theatre (LOCT), which was in a little church off of North Shore Road. The show was *The Pajama Game*. I was cast in the chorus, and it was great fun. My daughter worked backstage moving scenery, and my two sons directed cars, telling drivers where to park, as parking was very limited. I continued auditioning for several years after that and enjoyed being in shows. My brother and his wife and their three sons also got involved. When the LOCT president, Karen Conway, asked me if I would become the first producer of the theater, I told her I knew nothing about producing. She said she would teach me—and teach me she did. So began my career, which spanned more than 40 years, as executive producer of the LOCT (later Lakewood Theatre Company).

Along the way, I made many lifetime friends who were actors, musicians, technical specialists, volunteers, board members, and Lakewood staff. They became my second family.

When the Lakewood School building went up for sale, the theater's board of directors, executive director Andrew Edwards, and I knew it would be perfect for us. We all rolled up our shirtsleeves, and with the tremendous support of the greater Lake Oswego and Portland community, we were successful in buying the old school. Within a short time, the Lakewood auditorium was transitioned into a beautiful theater. It was such a huge improvement from the small space we had at the old church. We were able to do shows with bigger casts and have more musicians and greater technical support. But best of all, we were able to comfortably accommodate a larger audience. It was a dream come true!

With the additional space, we were able to provide studios for ballet, tap, aerobics, and piano classes, including a preschool that focused on the arts, and have classrooms for classes in the arts for adults and children. The lower level of the building became available for community groups, but we realized it could also be used for another theater space. It seemed that overnight, the once-tiny community theater became central to the arts in Lake Oswego. Early on, the building was busy every day of the week from morning until late at night. The community completely embraced Lakewood.

Over the years, Lakewood has touched thousands of lives, from children who were in their first show to audience members who count their favorite shows as having been performed on the Lakewood stage. The center has been the backdrop for family celebrations, wedding receptions, and memorials. Lakewood has always been a welcoming place for those who love the arts, and that is why so many continue to support Lakewood today.

—Kay Griffin Vega

ACKNOWLEDGMENTS

This book would not have been possible without the help of volunteers and staff members who archived thousands of historical documents along the way.

I would like to thank Steve and Lisa Knox, Andrew Edwards, Kay Griffin Vega, Mary Turnock, Kurt Herman, and Jackie Culver for sharing their personal stories and helping with photograph identification. I would to thank the Lake Oswego Library staff and volunteers who created the oral history interviews of the 1960s and 1970s. Much appreciation goes to Todd, Laura, and Marilyn at the Lake Oswego Library reference desk for help in obtaining historical photographs and articles. I would like to thank author/publisher/armchair historian Nancy Dunis for providing context and help in assuring the accuracy of this document. Thank you to my family and friends whose support made all the difference. I am most grateful to Arcadia Publishing editors Caroline (Anderson) Vickerson—for her support, guidance, and occasional nudge—and Sara Miller.

Unless otherwise noted, all images appearing in this book were graciously provided by Lakewood Theatre Company.

INTRODUCTION

The Oswego Players group, later known as the Lake Oswego Community Theatre and now called Lakewood Theatre Company, was founded by Emma Schiffer, Janice Gibbs, Jane Erikson, and Hap Young in 1952. Recollections of the group's early years were captured in an interview by Steve Turner, a reference librarian, and Theresa Truchot in 1973.

Schiffer recalls a small group having dinner and thinking it would be fun for the community to have "a little theater." So, they called together a larger group to meet at the home of Dorothy Peetz to discuss the possibility. The Oswego Players selected an ambitious play—a Noël Coward comedy, *Blithe Spirit*, which was "one of wordiest and most difficult plays to produce." Schiffer admitted that "all of us were nothing but ham actors, and one just loved playacting." Robert Orth, a young playwright and actor, was chosen as the Oswego Players director. After 10 days of rehearsals, the opening performance of *Blithe Spirit* was set to take place in the Lake Oswego High School cafeteria. The group agreed that the stage was "inadequate," but "we didn't know that either."

On May 15 and 16, 1953, the Oswego Players' first hilarious production boasted a talented cast. The leads were played by Al Cereghino and Lenore Martin. The Blithe Spirit, the first wife who haunts the main character about his second marriage, was played by Elizabeth "Liz" Weinel. Other cast members included John A. Topa (a Screen Actors Guild member), Gibbs, and Kay Powers, with Schiffer conducting séances as Madame Aracati. Behind the scenes were technical director James Nastasia, stage managers John Illo and Ernest Gibbs, costumer Betty Kingsbury, box office managers William and Marge Schwabe, makeup artists Dorothy Peetz and Win Nastasia, and a cadre of other crew members.

"We lived it, we breathed it, until the husbands almost got divorces from their wives and vice versa," says Schiffer. Preshow dinners for invited guests were held at the Oswego Country Club and hosted by Lee and Jacqueline "Jackie" Cosart. The crowd was enthusiastic. The show played for two nights, and the whole community was "buzzing that we now had a little theater."

In preparation for the next production, the Oswego Players held a variety of workshops and invited public participation. James Cameron of Portland Civic Theater and Margaret Barney of Fir Acres Theatre at Lewis & Clark College headed a panel discussion on theater technique. Kingsbury, the president of Oswego Players, presided over the discussion held at the Lake Oswego High School library. The next evening, a workshop was held by Gibbs and Illo to discuss stage lighting. At the time, the Oswego Players board leadership included Kingsbury serving as president, William Schwabe as vice president, Jean Avison as secretary, and Wilson Schiffer as treasurer. There were about 50 members.

The second Oswego Players show, the farce *Two Blind Mice*, was held at Lake Oswego High School on August 20, 21, and 22, 1953. The public was invited to audition, serve on committees, and participate in technical aspects of the production of *Two Blind Mice*. When some of the small roles remained unfilled, the Oswego Players made a second attempt, publishing a call in the local newspaper.

Director Scott Beach, a graduate of Lewis & Clark College, appeared in 16 plays at the college and was also involved in the Portland Civic Theatre. Beach won a Fulbright scholarship in music, which enabled him to study in France for a year. The cast of *Two Blind Mice* included Dorothy Jones from Portland Civic Theatre productions and Jan Gibbs, who had appeared in small theaters in San Diego and San Francisco. Other cast members included Gibson Kingsbury Jr., a student and actor at Portland State College; Dewey Harless of York Theatre Company based in Victoria, BC, Canada; and Liz Weinel, whose previous experience included playing Elvira in the Oswego Players' first production, *Blithe Spirit*.

The Oswego Players changed names to Lake Oswego Community Theatre (LOCT) in 1954. The group presented shows at the Odd Fellows Hall, Lewis & Clark College, Lakewood Elementary (later known as Lakewood School), Lake Oswego High and Junior High, and other venues. The Odd Fellows Hall was built at 295 Durham Street around 1890 and was used as a voting place for several years. The first Lake Oswego city elections were held there.

For the first eight years of its existence, the group had been limited to three productions per year, as they had to travel to various locations to put on a show. All of the schools at which they presented shows had their own drama departments with their own activities that required the use of their auditoriums, and the Odd Fellows Hall hosted community meetings and elections, among other activities. The lack of a dedicated performance space limited the number of productions LOCT was able to stage. The acquisition of a theater building would enable the group to double the number of productions.

According to Emma Schiffer, "We finally knew that the time had come when we had to have a home of our own, because no longer could we be bounced around from pillar to post and have a theater. We had to have a home with room to expand and the security that we needed." Jane Erikson agreed: "We had to have a home or disband." This led to the start of a fundraising campaign in 1961 and a search for a permanent home. The group had not yet solicited patrons, but now they would try to raise a little money.

However, the group's fundraising plans were hindered by current and former presidents either leaving or resigning. Fred Ebeling, who had served as president from 1957 to 1958, moved to Denver. Jewell Gallagher, president from 1958 to 1959, moved to North Carolina. Helen Mills, president from 1959 to 1960, resigned. Cid Hord, president from 1960 to 1961, moved his business activities to Salem, Oregon.

On June 30, 1960, the *Oswego Review* reported that "the entire present board turned in their resignations but there was sufficient interest that a new interim board was appointed." At the LOCT membership meeting on June 23, 1960, a statement was read by Weinel, the board secretary, stating that "lack of community interest in attending and casting plays were given as the reasons." Then-president Mills had signed the statement. The *Oswego Review* also reported that there was "some discussion of a solution to the third play planned [that] could not be presented in May when scheduled. The reason was inability to cast it." The interim board members charged with reorganizing LOCT included Cid Hord (chairman), Emma Schiffer, Jane Erickson, Bill Chandler, Ann Olsen, and Lucille Knox.

Coincidentally, a new dance studio that also featured plays opened in January 1958 a half mile away in the Oswego Marina building: Catherine Cassarno's Marina Theatre of Oswego. After the group staged *Nude with Violin* and *The Chalk Garden*, Marina Theatre of Oswego's third production, *Make a Million*, opened on June 16, 1960, with Paul Ouellette as the director, Jim Erickson as the lighting operator, and Roald B. Wulff as one of the actors—all of whom were longtime LOCT associates. It became Ballet du Lac in 1962, under the direction of Cassarno, and was a member of the National Ballet Association.

Jane Erikson had an idea after seeing the Traveling Bishops perform at the old Methodist church just off of State Street. She thought it was "a very nice place to give a play." A new Methodist church had been built on South Shore Road, so Erikson called the minister and asked if the old church building was for sale. The minister said that it was for sale and encouraged Erikson to contact Carl Rohde for details. The price was $15,000. LOCT had $300 in the bank.

Erikson created a slogan after a visit to the church: "We found the church, now we would have to find the angels." That same year, all three presidents of LOCT had moved out of town. Hap Young suggested that a lawyer, Paul Bullier, should join the board. "That was the luckiest thing that ever happened to the Lake Oswego Community Theatre," said Erikson, as Bullier helped with all legal and tax matters. "Without Paul, we would never have a theater."

None of the founders really knew much about fundraising. Erikson pointed out that raising money for a park or a hospital is relatively easy considering it benefits everyone. But a theater was much different. She said, "If you find 1 person in about 40 who is really enthusiastic and wants to give up a lot of money—you are very lucky."

The group raised about $28 dollars in the beginning. Dwayne Autzen from the Autzen Foundation wrote a check for $500, and Erikson "nearly fainted" because that was the largest amount the group had been able to get. In April 1961, Jim Callas, then the president of LOCT, and Paul Murphy Jr., chairman of the building fundraising drive, set a goal of raising $10,000. As part of the drive, LOCT had held a tea fundraiser; the intent was not only to raise money but to allow patrons to explore the building and let their imaginations run wild as they envisioned how to create a cultural center in that location.

Carl Rohde gave the group a 30-day extension, and at the end of 90 days, they had raised $6,000. A lot of the donations were given in cash in the form of $1 bills. Erikson was about to tell the minister that they had not raised enough money and would back out of the pending sale. It had been understood from the beginning that the church would not take a mortgage on the balance. Then, the minister said, "We could use $6,000 in cash, and we'll take it." On October 24, 1961, the Lake Oswego Community Theatre officially owned the old Methodist church building and therefore had a home.

Theater activities included children's plays, adult acting workshops, and a series of art films. About 65 people could sit in the 100-year-old church pews. The building did not have air-conditioning. One of the directors, Greg Tamblyn, was known to use a bucket of ice water to splash the audience during the summer. The main floor was eventually converted into a seating area that fit about 100. Refreshments were prepared in the basement kitchen area. Over 110 productions were staged at the location from 1961 to 1979. The first show held in the church (prior to LOCT owning it) was *The Pleasure of His Company*, with Lucille Knox playing the lead. *Arsenic and Old Lace* was the first play performed after LOCT owned the church.

The old Methodist church on Greenwood Road proved to be a good investment, leading to a growing membership and sold-out performances, but its space was limited. So, when Lakewood School, located at 368 S. State Street, became available in 1979, the board seized the opportunity, and the idea of a community center for the arts began to take shape. Bill Headlee, the board president, emphasized financial caution.

After a successful fundraising campaign chaired by Ed Hart, LOCT decided to buy the Lakewood School building from Lake Oswego School District. On December 4, 1980, the Lake Oswego Design Review Board gave LOCT the approval to convert Lakewood School to Lakewood Center for the Arts, a nonprofit community cultural center. The original purchase price was $600,000. By January 1982, a total of $108,750 had been spent on facility improvements.

In 1977, theater manager Andrew Edwards became the first paid employee at Lake Oswego Community Theatre. Two years later, he became executive director of the Lakewood Center for the Arts. Under his leadership, several improvements were made to the Lakewood Center, including the creation of two art galleries, a preschool program, and dance studios, as well as the renovation of a community meeting room.

The first LOCT production, held at Lakewood School's gymnasium in 1980, was *Snow White at the Circus*, directed by Stan Foote and Sahni Samuelson. At this time, LOCT was still presenting shows in the old Methodist church location just behind the Lakewood Center; the last show performed at the church was *Bedroom Farce* in March 1983.

The Lakewood Center building was paid for in full in 1987 with help from a successful capital campaign that raised over $1 million. Many changes took place during the 1980s, including the start of the citywide Lake Oswego Festival of the Arts, managed by the Lakewood Center for the Arts. The festival brings together approximately 25,000 people annually with a focus on arts education, performances, and exhibitions.

In 1990, to celebrate its 10th year at the Lakewood Center, Lake Oswego Community Theatre officially became the Lakewood Theatre Company.

In 2003, Lakewood Theatre Company, doing business as Lakewood Center for the Arts, completed a $3 million project to build a new stage house with a remodeled 220-seat theater. Lakewood Theatre Company honored the Headlee family by renaming it Headlee Mainstage in 2003.

The old Methodist church on Greenwood Road came up for sale, again for $600,000, but then the price dropped to $300,000, and longtime board member Bill Warner thought it might be a good idea to repurchase it and use it for rehearsal space. After some discussion, the board decided that the space was not conducive to running rehearsals. It was not the same size as the main stage, and they did not want to burden the crew with moving supplies back and forth.

A plan was put in motion to replace part of the Lakewood School's former playground with a replica of the Headlee Mainstage that could be used as a dedicated rehearsal space. Built in 2015, the 40-by-50-foot Artist Training Facility (later renamed Warner Hall as a dedication to Bill and Barbara Warner) could be used for rehearsals and leased for other classes and programs. Theater membership has continued to grow to over 2,000, and more than 500 productions have been completed on the Headlee Mainstage and the lower-level Side Door Stage.

In March 2020, the novel coronavirus (COVID-19) pandemic shuttered theater venues around the globe. The first case in Oregon was announced on February 28, 2020—an employee at Lake Oswego's Forest Hills Elementary had contracted the virus. Local officials took steps to minimize the spread.

Lakewood Theatre Company was forced to close its doors to visitors during its 68th performance season. Shows were postponed or canceled. Classes were held remotely. Fundraising was moved online, with livestreaming of the annual *Lakewood in City Lights* auction event. After 18 long months, Lakewood Theatre Company finally reopened with a live performance of *The Odd Couple* on September 23, 2021.

One

MEET THE FOUNDERS

OSWEGO PLAYERS. From left to right are Oswego Players founders Jane Erikson, Emma Schiffer, Jan Gibbs, and Hap Young, with language associates technician Robert Simpson standing behind the group. They were interviewed for the bicentennial oral history project published as "In Their Own Words" in 1973. (Courtesy of Lake Oswego Library.)

DOROTHY PEETZ. In the fall of 1952, 16 people gathered in the basement recreation room at the home of Peetz, an instructor of core academics at Lake Oswego High School. The original company of Oswego Players included actors and playwrights like Betty and Gibson Kingsbury, Emma and Wilson Schiffer, Jean Avison, William and Marge Schwabe, John and Lillian Finlay, Kay Powers, Jane Erickson, Liz Weinel, and Jacqueline and Lee Cosart. Later, the group's meetings were held at the home of the Cosarts. One single element welded them together: a love of theater. Experience was not required to join the theater group—only interest. The group's purpose was to establish a community theater for Lake Oswego. It was a gamble; at that time, few communities in Oregon had successfully supported a theater group. (Courtesy of Lake Oswego Library.)

BETTY KINGSBURY. The first president of the Oswego Players, Betty Kingsbury, served from 1952 to 1953 and offered people of all ages the opportunity to learn the many facets of play production free of charge: acting, costuming, lighting, set design, makeup, publicity, staging, and stage management. The handful of energetic members who organized the Lake Oswego Players had a vision for the little theater. The all-volunteer group thought the beautiful lake area was an ideal setting for a small but busy civic center that would prove its worth to its people. Kingsbury presided over board elections and committees, organized preshow dinners, and encouraged local theater professionals to participate in panel discussions and workshops at the Lake Oswego High School library. In the beginning, the group's tentative plan was to put on two shows per year at Lake Oswego High School. (Courtesy of Lake Oswego Library.)

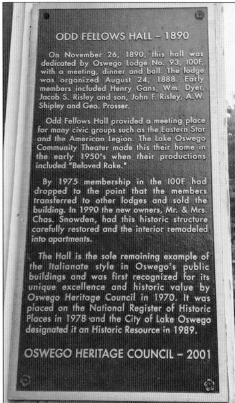

ODD FELLOWS HALL – 1890

On November 26, 1890, this hall was dedicated by Oswego Lodge No. 93, IOOF, with a meeting, dinner and ball. The lodge was organized August 24, 1888. Early members included Henry Gans, Wm. Dyer, Jacob S. Risley and son, John F. Risley, A.W. Shipley and Geo. Prosser.

Odd Fellows Hall provided a meeting place for many civic groups such as the Eastern Star and the American Legion. The Lake Oswego Community Theater made this their home in the early 1950's when their productions included "Beloved Rake."

By 1975 membership in the IOOF had dropped to the point that the members transferred to other lodges and sold the building. In 1990 the new owners, Mr. & Mrs. Chas. Snowden, had this historic structure carefully restored and the interior remodeled into apartments.

The Hall is the sole remaining example of the Italianate style in Oswego's public buildings and was first recognized for its unique excellence and historic value by Oswego Heritage Council in 1970. It was placed on the National Register of Historic Places in 1978 and the City of Lake Oswego designated it an Historic Resource in 1989.

OSWEGO HERITAGE COUNCIL – 2001

ODD FELLOWS HALL. The Odd Fellows Hall was built around 1890 and listed in the National Register of Historic Places in 1978. Without a permanent place to call their own, the Oswego Players performed in the Odd Fellows Hall. Founder Emma Schiffer described the building as having "so many stairs to get up to the second floor. The time that we had really big crowds we were all scared to death that the building was going to collapse with the weight. The stairs squeaked. The dressing room was just a sheet hanging between the restrooms." The four-by-four-foot dressing room space was shared with sometimes up to 20 people of all ages who had to change costumes from start to finish of a production. The bathroom was very noisy. The space rattled. During intermission, the patrons would have coffee downstairs. "It was hysterical," Schiffer said. "We had more fun than the patrons." The first play held at the Odd Fellows Hall was *Claudia* in 1954. The photograph at left is the historical marker for the Odd Fellows Hall. (Above, courtesy of Lake Oswego Library; left, author's collection.)

BLITHE SPIRIT. The Oswego Players presented their first production on May 15 and 16, 1953, under the direction of high school teacher Robert Orth. The group selected the Noël Coward comedy *Blithe Spirit.* After 10 days of rehearsals, the opening performance was set to be held in the Lake Oswego High School cafeteria. A small fundraising project collected $28, and the show went into production. According to Oswego Players founder Emma Schiffer: "We put on this show to a very enthusiastic group, and we played it for two nights. The whole community was buzzing that we now had a little theater."

Lake Oswego Players

PRESENT

TWO BLIND MICE
by S spewack

DIRECTED BY A. SCOTT BEACH
LAKE OSWEGO HIGH SCHOOL CAFE
AUGUST 20, 21, 22   8:30 P.M.

TWO BLIND MICE. This playbill was handed to attendees of the Oswego Players' second production, *Two Blind Mice*, in August 1953. The show was a farce about the subject of "government, red tape, bureaucracy, love and the lives of people of Washington, DC." It was held at the Lake Oswego High School cafeteria. The director, Scott Beach, graduated from Lewis & Clark College and appeared in 16 plays there; he was also involved in the Portland Civic Theatre. The cast included Dorothy Jones, Jan Gibbs, Gibson Kingsbury Jr., Dewey Harless, and Liz Weinel (who previously appeared as Elvira in the Oswego Players' first production, *Blithe Spirit*). Other cast members included Jim Nastasia, John Illo, Dr. John Finlay, Ernest Gibbs, Dale Liberty, Dole Pearson, Don Finlay, and Don Foss.

PENNY WISE. This show first opened on New York City's Broadway in 1937; the play's setting is the Penny Wise Farm in Connecticut, and the playwright is Jean Ferguson Black. It is a story about what happens when three mistresses show up at a philanderer's vacation farmhouse and become friends with his wife. This 1954 Oswego Players' production of *Penny Wise* was performed in the Lake Oswego High School cafeteria. Pictured here are Liz Weinel (left) and Paul Casebeer.

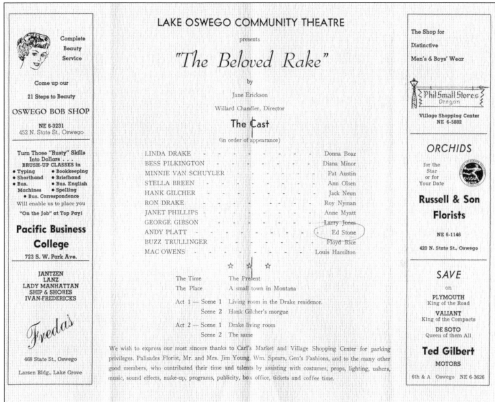

LAKE OSWEGO COMMUNITY THEATRE

presents

"*The Beloved Rake*"

by

Jane Erickson

Willard Chandler, Director

The Cast

(in order of appearance)

LINDA DRAKE	Donna Boaz
BESS PILKINGTON	Diana Minor
MINNIE VAN SCHUYLER	Pat Austin
STELLA BREEN	Ann Olsen
HANK GILCHER	Jack Neun
RON DRAKE	Roy Nyman
JANET PHILLIPS	Anne Myatt
GEORGE GIBSON	Larry Jones
ANDY PLATT	Ed Stone
BUZZ TRULLINGER	Floyd Rice
MAC OWENS	Louis Hamilton

☆   ☆   ☆

The Time	The Present
The Place	A small town in Montana
Act 1 — Scene 1	Living room in the Drake residence.
Scene 2	Hank Gilcher's morgue
Act 2 — Scene 1	Drake living room
Scene 2	The same

We wish to express our most sincere thanks to Carl's Market and Village Shopping Center for parking privileges. Palisades Florist, Mr. and Mrs. Jim Young, Wm. Spears, Gen's Fashions, and to the many other good members, who contributed their time and talents by assisting with costumes, props, lighting, ushers, music, sound effects, make-up, programs, publicity, box office, tickets and coffee time.

THE BELOVED RAKE. Written by award-winning playwright and Oswego Players founder Jane Erickson, the first production of the 1960–1961 season was a huge comedy hit performed in the Odd Fellows Hall. The play became the most successful produced by the group to date. The teaching staff at Lake Oswego Junior High was well represented by Anne Myatt and Ed Stone. Ann Olsen made her first local appearance as inquisitive and persistent reporter Stella Breen.

THE HOME OF RUDOLPH AND JANE ERICKSON. Lake Oswego's own playwright Jane Erickson spent many hours writing in this bungalow-style home built in 1920 at 2535 Glenmorrie Drive. Her husband, Rudolph, may have wondered why writing a comedy about a funeral was considered a good idea. The Oswego Players became the Lake Oswego Community Theatre during this time (in 1954) and presented the world premiere of Jane Erickson's *The Beloved Rake* in 1955 at the Odd Fellows Hall. Jane wrote the play while taking a writing seminar from Dr. Charles Guapp at Reed College and edited it based on feedback. Among the plays written by Jane is *A Mighty Fortress*, a historical play about Marcus and Narcissa Whitman, which was successfully produced many times around the United States. Her other plays include *Porcupine Steaks* and *Go Ahead Joe Meek*. (Courtesy of Lake Oswego Library.)

SEVEN NUNS AT LAS VEGAS. From left to right are Peaches (played by former Powers model Patti Ebeling), Boots (played by Carole Kirkpatrick), Baby (played by Donna Clampitt), and Sister Anne (played by Mimi Haggerty). Directed by Lake Oswego Community Theatre's past president Cecil Matson, a Lake Oswego High School drama teacher, the play begins with seven nuns from Indiana who find themselves in the Las Vegas nightclub business. This comedy was the first play of the Lake Oswego Community Theatre's 1957–1958 season. The Queen of the Immaculate Conception circle of Our Lady of the Lake church sold tickets for opening night. Curtain time was 8:30 p.m., and admission was $1.25 for adults and 75¢ for students. The drama and speech department of Oswego Junior High School benefitted from the profits of this production.

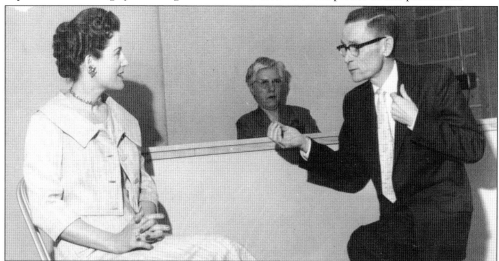

NIGHT OF JANUARY 16TH. Pictured here are, from left to right, Mimi Haggerty (as the secretary on trial), Marion Kelso (as the judge), and Fred Ebeling (as the defense counsel). In May 1958, Lake Oswego Community Theatre concluded the 1957–1958 season with *Night of January 16th* at Lake Oswego Junior High School. Haggerty's character was on trial for the death and disappearance of the Swedish Match King, and Ebeling's attorney character defended her. Joe Shobe, the Clackamas County sheriff, summoned audience members to fill the jury box every night, and the play's ending depended on these unrehearsed jury verdicts.

THE OSWEGO COMMUNITY THEATRE
EXPRESSES THEIR APPRECIATION . . .

Lakeside Lumber · · · · · · · · · Lumber

Oswego Review · · · · · · · · · Publicity

Lakewood Elementary School · · · · · · Building

Lewis and Clark · · · · · · · · Properties

Oswego Lodge · · · · · · · · · Props

Mr. and Mrs. John Davie · · · · · · · Sponsor

Mrs. Jane Erickson · · · · · · · · Sponsor

Mrs. Betty Kingsbury · · · · · · · · Sponsor

lake oswego community theatre

Presents

I   THE STRONGER

By August Strinberg

II   A PHOENIX TOO FREQUENT

By Christopher Fry

TWO ONE-ACT PLAYS

Directed by Willard Chandler

Lakewood Elementary School
Oswego, Oregon
November 13, 14 & 20, 21, 1959

THE STRONGER AND A PHOENIX TOO FREQUENT. Lake Oswego Community Theatre playbills were distributed to eager crowds at the start of these two one-act plays performed in the Lakewood Elementary School gymnasium in 1959. The theater group may not have envisioned that years later, this gymnasium would become the home of the Headlee Mainstage. *The Stronger*, written by August Strinberg, was set in Paris on a clear winter day and starred Lanni Hurst as Mrs. X and Rosemary May as Miss X. *A Phoenix Too Frequent*, written by Christopher Fry, begins in a small dark tomb outside the walled city of Ephensus in 1 AD. The cast included Barbara Lewis as Doto, Lucille Knox as Dynamene, and Thomas Hayes as Tegeus. Directed by Willard Chandler, these performances kicked off the 1959–1960 season and took place on November 13, 14, 20, and 21. One performance took place at the Portland Yacht Club and included an unexpected actor as a "corpse," which did not throw off the cast but did surprise the director.

THE BISHOP MISBEHAVES. In 1960, the Oswego Players produced *The Bishop Misbehaves*, a comedy in three acts, by Frederick J. Jackson. Lady Emily was played by Lake Oswego High School English teacher Joanna Jeffries. Other cast members are unidentified. The play was performed in the Lake Grove Elementary School gymnasium, which challenged the theater company, as it had to be transformed into a stunning medieval palace. The settings are a British pub, the Queen's Head, at Tadworth in Surrey, and the Hall of the Bishop's Palace at Broadminster. As the story goes, the bishop of Broadminster and his sister walk into a pub, and it is curiously quiet. After a look around, they find three people bound and gagged in the closet and listen to their ordeal of being robbed of their jewels and wallet. The bishop, a fan of detective fiction, dreamed of being a Scotland Yard man, so he is thrilled to help solve the crime.

SUSPECT. In 1961, the cast of *Suspect* performed in the Odd Fellows Hall. The audience appears as the background to the performance. The stage follows a thrust design, with the audience located on three sides of the stage and only a few feet away from the action. Some members of the audience would look at other audience members across the stage, taking the focus off of the production. Managing the set changes and special effects was a challenge, since the hall lacked an extended stage area. The scenery could not be more than a few feet tall so it did not block audience views. This location, which was less than ideal, put major restrictions on the theater company.

Two

LAKE OSWEGO
COMMUNITY THEATRE

OLD METHODIST CHURCH. The old Methodist church, built in 1896, was moved down a hill—using ropes and rollers—to its present site in 1928. The building has many features characteristic of Queen Anne–style architecture from the late 19th century and served as one of the first churches in Oswego. Jane Erickson thought it was "a very nice place to give a play" after seeing the Traveling Bishops perform here. (Courtesy of Lake Oswego Library.)

THE PLEASURE OF HIS COMPANY. In May and June 1961, *The Pleasure of His Company* took center stage at the old Methodist church. On May 11, 1961, an article in the Oswego Review stated: "When the curtain goes up on *The Pleasure of His Company*, the Lake Oswego Community Theatre production, Thursday, May 25, audiences will be given a first-hand preview of things to come. The play will be presented in the building the theatre group hopes to make its permanent home, the former Oswego Methodist church off State Street, on Greenwood Road. Having secured an option on the church building, the community theatre hopes to be able to purchase it and make necessary changes through the building fund drive which is now underway." The play takes place at a house on the hills of San Francisco. It is about Pogo (played by Larry Kott), an estranged father who returns for his daughter's wedding. The daughter (played by Leslie Nyman) enjoys spending time with her father and begins to think that her fiancé is unsophisticated. Pogo is still smitten with his ex-wife Katherine (played by Lucille Knox), although she is married to Jim (played by John Hughes). Eventually, the charming Pogo leaves without breaking up either couple. Kott also starred in *Sabrina Fair*. Offstage, Kott (pictured) was known to 15,000 primary schoolchildren as "Larry from Alpenrose Dairy."

Our Cast

JAN GIBBS, always a sparkling addition to any play, is no stranger to LOCT audiences. She appeared in its first play, "Blithe Spirit" and last in "Seven Nuns in Las Vegas," and many in between. Her hobbies are "re-doing" furniture and "undoing" grandchildren.

PAT GILLETT spends most of her time charming first graders at Wilsonville grade school. Pat was once a "Miss Brewster" sans poisons. A welcome newcomer to our group.

DR. JOHN FINLAY is as pleasant off-stage as the real Boris Karloff. A well-known dentist, and veteran of such Oswego productions as "My Three Angels" and "Two Blind Mice."

KEN GOODALL is another "alum" from "My Three Angels" and he also appeared in the first production of "Beloved Rake." Off-stage, Ken is a familiar figure to customers of Goodall Oil Company.

ALAN WANLESS is an Oswego "find" who is appearing in his third consecutive show for us, the others being "You Touched Me" and "The Pleasure of His Company."

PHYLLIS SPEROS makes her debut here, but has directed or acted in nearly thirty productions with the Bend Plays, Portland Civic Theater and Lewis & Clark College.

BERT GILLETT, the husband of "Martha," is another newcomer to our group. Off-stage he teaches eighth grae at Turner Grade School.

JACK LEE POWELL teaches English, coaches swimming, and teaches drama at Oswego High Sschool, and is also the proud father of the school's new stage. Past roles include "Make a Million" and "Ten Little Indians."

ED STONE is making his second appearance with us, his first being in "Beloved Rake." He teaches math and science at the Junior High School and plans to go into speech therapy.

RALPH PETERSON is making his first acting appearance in this play, but he is an old hand at minstrel shows. Any resemblance to a teddy-bear is purely Ralph.

ERNIE GIBBS is well-known to Oswegoans and has always been a favorite—back stage, front stage and off stage. He not only has been in many shows here and at Civic, but is past president of LOCT.

GARY KINGSBURY is following in his parents' footsteps as a LOCT actor. This marks his first appearance, but we hope not his last.

STAN GIROD is a grade school vice principal in the Lake Oswego District.

We wish to express our most sincere thanks to Carl's Market and Village Shopping Center for parking privileges; to Althea's Attic and Marylhurst College for furniture and properties; to our production manager, Roy Nyman; stage manager, Hilda Jackson; properties, Gretchen Henkle; hospitality, Mrs. August Weinel; costumes, Mrs. Betty Kingsbury; and Carol Day, publicity, and to the many others who assisted them.

ARSENIC AND OLD LACE. When the curtain rose on Lake Oswego Community Theatre's production of *Arsenic and Old Lace* on November 24, 1961, it was the first performance after the group's purchase of the old Methodist church at 156 Greenwood Road. This program featured biographies of the LOCT cast of this classic comedy. The hero, Mortimer Brewster (played by Ken Goodall), is a drama critic who must deal with his crazy, homicidal family and local police in Brooklyn, New York, as he decides whether to go through with his promise to marry the woman he loves, Elaine Harper (played by Phyllis Speros), who lives next door and is the daughter of the local minister. His family includes two spinster aunts, Abby and Martha Brewster (played by Jan Gibbs and Pat Gillett, respectively), who took to murdering lonely old men by poisoning them with a glass of homemade elderberry wine laced with arsenic, strychnine, and "just a pinch" of cyanide.

SABRINA FAIR. From left to right are (first row) Cliff Gorman (who played David Larrabee), Jana Kieper (who played Sabrina Fair), and Larry Kott (who played Linus Larrabee Jr.); (second row) Betty Peterson (who played Maude Larrabee) and Murray Lockard (who played Linus Larrabee Sr.). *Sabrina Fair* is a romantic comedy set in 1950s Long Island. Lake Oswego Community Theatre held performances of the play at the old Methodist church at 156 Greenwood Road in 1962.

JANA KIEPER AS SABRINA FAIR. Sabrina Fair is a charming, well-educated girl who just happens to be the daughter of hired help and then becomes the love interest of two sons from the wealthy Larrabee family. The boys' mother, Maude Larrabee, is exasperated by the situation, and their father, Linus Larrabee Sr., entertains himself by attending funerals. In the end, Sabrina chooses to be with the cold businessman–turned–loving Linus Jr. (played by Larry Kott). The play is a fun escape from the garden variety Cinderella story.

BOB BUSEICK. Bob Buseick, who directed the Lake Oswego Community Theatre production of Samuel Taylor's *Sabrina Fair* in 1962, was a well-known actor in the Portland and Oswego areas. His biography in the play's program read: "He juggles acting, directing, studying, and teaching. He is a Drama teacher at the Junior High. Wife Jan and three little Buseicks do see him occasionally." He later added "playwright" to his repertoire. He became drama director at Beaverton High School and served as a member of the Lake Oswego Community Theatre board of directors. He and his family moved to Shreveport, Louisiana, in 1969. He spent 36 years as chair of the Department of Theatre and Dance at Centenary College of Louisiana. His play *My Sister in This House* was performed at the Kennedy Center in Washington, DC.

GHOSTS. In 1962, the Lake Oswego Community Theatre production of Henrik Ibsen's *Ghosts* was controversial and took the theater company out of its comfort zone of comedy. The play starred Lanni Hurst as Helene Alving (right) and Bob Buseick as Oswald Alving. Hurst was very active in the Portland theater scene and instrumental in the campaign to save the old Methodist church. *Ghosts* was written in the late 1880s. Ibsen's realistic theater revolutionized the thought patterns of men and women. Today, *Ghosts* has taken its place in the history of dramatic literature. Mailed postcards, like the one shown below, encouraged theater members to see the show.

L O C T ANNOUNCES:

HENRIK IBSEN'S COMPELLING, SUSPENSE- FILLED DRAMA

GHOSTS

FEATURING

LANNIE HURST as Mrs. Alving

BOB BUSEICK as Oswald   **MARY SMITH as Regina**

LARRY KOTT as Pastor Manders   **GARY LANSING as Engstrand**

DIRECTED BY KEN WATERS   *EXECUTIVE DIRECTOR, BEN PADROW*

May 18-19, 25-26, and June 1-2 -   8:30 p. m.

Lake Oswego Community Theatre

156 Greenwood Road   Call NE6-3296 for reservations

Lake Oswego Community Theatre
156 GREENWOOD ROAD
LAKE OSWEGO, OREGON

Bob Buseick as Oswald Alving in *Ghosts*. Set in the 1800s, the drama takes place on Helene Alving's country estate on one of the fjords in the west of Norway. In the course of the play, Helene discovers that her son Oswald is suffering from syphilis. She also discovers that Oswald has fallen in love with her maid Regina Engstrand, who is revealed to be the illegitimate daughter of her husband, Captain Alving, and therefore Oswald's half-sister. The play concludes with Helene having to decide whether to euthanize her son in accordance with his wishes. Although the subject matter was considered "revolting" by some early critics upon release, the play portrayed life as it really was. Bob Buseick appeared in many Lake Oswego Community Theatre productions, including *Dial M for Murder*. He also performed at the Portland Civic Auditorium in *Toys in the Attic*.

BELL, BOOK AND CANDLE. From left to right are (first row) Gary Lansing and Joan Reynolds; (second row) Jim Smith, Evelyn Zilka, and Ben Padrow. In 1962, radio show producer and Lake Oswego Community Theatre actress Ann Olsen wrote, "The Lake Oswego Community Theatre, up to its bell tower in witchcraft these days, is brewing up a particularly palatable potion of fun and fantasy entitled *Bell, Book and Candle*." It is the story of a witch named Gillian Holroyd (played by Reynolds), who casts a spell on her love interest Shepard Henderson (played by Lansing). Aiding Gillian are her brother Nicky (played by Smith) and aunt Queenie (played by Zilka), who are not above throwing a few private hexes of their own. Padrow, Lake Oswego Community Theatre's executive director and a professor at Portland State College, played author Sidney Redlitch. Olsen also said, "Mastermind of all this stagecraft sorcery is director Paul Ouellette, whose reputation for the 'magic touch' in theater is known all over the Northwest." Ouellette served as chairman of the speech and drama department at the University of Portland.

MARY MAURER SMITH AS CANDIDA. Smith starred as Candida in this 1962 production at Lake Oswego Community Theatre. *Candida* is a play by George Bernard Shaw about love and marriage in Victorian England. Candida must choose between a lovestruck poet, who has come to swoon her away from a dull family life, and her husband, the clergyman. Smith, the actor, did not have a dull family life. She came to Lake Oswego with a wealth of experience that included acting, dancing, directing, and singing in both New York and Hollywood. She has worked with the Strolling Players, the Players Ring in Hollywood, and the Masquer's Workshop. She appeared in the Lake Oswego Community Theatre's production of *Ghosts* and directed *Dial M for Murder*. Professionally, she was a teacher of English and speech at Lake Oswego High School. She was married to Clete Smith, advertising manager for White Stag, Portland's iconic apparel manufacturer.

CANDIDA. Pictured below are, from left to right, Robert Coffey (as Eugene Marchbanks), Rosemary Phipps (as Miss Proserpine Garnett), Mary Maurer Smith (as Candida), Herb Smith (as Rev. James Morell), and Jim Lloyd (as Rev. Alexander Mill). At left is the playbill for *Candida*, which featured the old Methodist church that became home to Lake Oswego Community Theatre, where the show was performed in 1962. The Lake Oswego Community Theatre playbill covers featured the old Methodist church building from 1961 to 1965.

GIGI. Miriam McNaughton (left) and Jan Gibbs are pictured here. Produced by Lake Oswego Community Theatre in 1963, *Gigi* is about a young 19th-century Parisian girl being groomed for high society by her aunt and grandmother. McNaughton (who played Aunt Alicia) appeared in productions at Seattle Repertory Theatre. Gibbs (who played Mamita) was one of the original founders of the Oswego Players, serving as vice president in 1954 and 1955 and starring in the group's first two productions. On Broadway, *Gigi* was Audrey Hepburn's breakout performance in 1952.

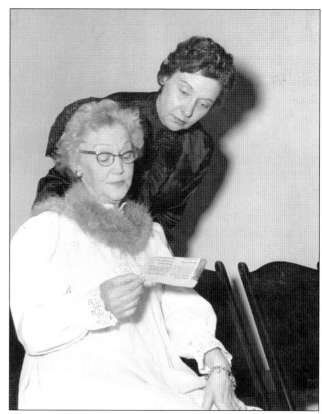

Gigi

Expenditure

Scripts	10.00	
"	1.25	
Royalties	110.00	
§ Dir. Fee	75.00	
Policing	10.00	
	206.25	

To come
Costumes	33.00
Dir. Fee	75.00
Policing	20.00

§ 334.25   plus others

Income   Admissions   § 144.70   (One weekend)

Outstanding Bills

Apex Elec. & Plumbing	7.34
Pacific Costumers	25.00
Goodwill	8.00
Stagecraft	197.50
Lloyds Lighting Supplies	95.00

BUDGET OF *GIGI.* The staff and volunteers at Lake Oswego Community Theatre did not let a limited budget discourage them. Early performances held at the old Methodist church were literally enjoyed "on the edge of your seat." The pews were constructed with square nails in 1894, around the same time as the building. About 65 people could sit in the pews with little comfort. The hard pews were later replaced with 124 upholstered seats purchased from Portland Civic Auditorium.

35

SOUTH PACIFIC. Lakewood School principal Stan Girod added his comedic and vocal talents to the 30-plus cast of *South Pacific* in 1963. Girod played Luther Billis, the sailor who takes up making grass skirts to sell. This production of the Rodgers and Hammerstein musical was under the direction of Jack Lee Powell, who also directed the drama and fine arts department and musicals at Lake Oswego High School. Jim Erickson, the associate director, was in charge of choreography and designed the set to transport the audience to an exotic paradise.

Trisha DuBay. Trisha DuBay (formerly Patti Piper) sang "I'm Gonna Wash That Man Right Outa My Hair" in the leading role of Nellie Forbush in *South Pacific* in 1963. DuBay had recently completed a USO tour of Eastern Asia. With all of the talent performing on one stage, this production of *South Pacific* became one of the most memorable performances held at Lake Oswego Community Theatre at 156 Greenwood Road.

Bus Stop. Directed by Miriam McNaughton and John Herbst Jr. in 1963, *Bus Stop* featured Mike Booth (left) as local sheriff Will Masters, John Uppinghouse (center) as ranch hand Virgil Blessing, and Dan Petter (right) as a cowboy. The action of the play takes place in a street-corner restaurant in a small town about 30 miles west of Kansas City. Offstage, Uppinghouse was also a sculptor, and his piece called *Fairy Tree* is part of the permanent collection at George Rogers Park, adjacent to the Iron Furnace.

DIAL M FOR MURDER. From left to right are Frank Faro (as Tony Wendice), Larry Kott (as Captain Lesgate), Peggy Cooke (as Margot Wendice), Bob Buseick (as Max Halliday), and David Jackson (as Inspector Hubbard). *Dial M for Murder* opened on February 28, 1964, and ran every Friday and Saturday night until March 21 of that year. The leading roles were played by Cooke, the head nurse at the medical school hospital, and Buseick, a drama teacher at Lake Oswego Junior High and a member of the Lake Oswego Community Theatre board of directors. Other cast members included Faro, a radio personality, and Jackson, a professor of biochemistry at the University of Oregon. Ed Gross, who played Thompson, worked in industrial sales with Pacific Chemical Company. Kott's cast biography reads: "A versatile actor and one of Lake Oswego's more eligible bachelors." Directing this industrious cast was Mary Maurer Smith, who was a speech and English teacher at Lake Oswego High School in 1964.

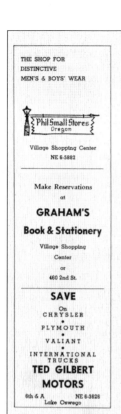

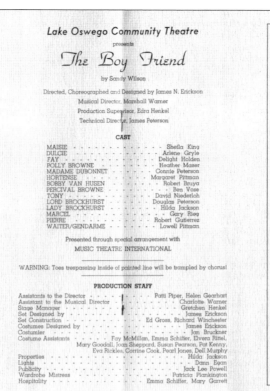

THE BOY FRIEND. The warning printed inside this playbill for the 1964 production of *The Boy Friend* says, "Toes trespassing inside of painted line will be trampled by chorus!" Although the group made many improvements to the building after purchasing it, the limited space led to the need to insert comical warnings for the audience. Patrons, advertisers, subscribers, and theatergoers provided the funds for comfortable new seating, professional lighting equipment, and a new piano. This same financial support—plus volunteer labor—accomplished the remodeling of the downstairs area to provide a pleasant social room, an efficient set-building room, a prop and costume room, and two connected dressing rooms. David Niederloh (right) played the role of Tony in this production.

AUNTIE MAME. From left to right are John Uppinghouse (as Ito), Hilda Jackson (as Vera Charles), Edra Henkel (as Norah Muldoon), Steve Knox (as Patrick Dennis), Mike Booth (as Lindsay Woolsey), and Lanni Hurst (as Auntie Mame). *Auntie Mame* is the story of a boy who is orphaned and sent to live with his eccentric aunt in the big city. Bob Buseick directed the 1964 production, and perhaps he inspired the young actor, as this marked the first LOCT performance by current Lakewood Theatre Company executive producer Steve Knox, who still remembers his lines: "Stir, never shake, bruises the gin." Knox said he always lived by those words. His biography in the program says: "A student at Lake Oswego Junior High School, young Steve has appeared in productions of *Heidi, Toad of Toad Hall, Alice in Wonderland, Peter Pan, The Innocence, Winnie the Pooh, and Androcles and the Lion.* He is a football and basketball player at Lake Oswego Junior High School. We hope he'll be back with us at Lake Oswego Community Theatre many times in the future."

41

Auntie Mame Takes Agnes under Her Wing. From left to right are John Uppinghouse (as Ito), Edra Henkel (as Norah Muldoon), Jan Bruckner (as Agnes Gooch), and Lanni Hurst (as Auntie Mame). The play is a madcap romp that takes place in Auntie Mame's Beekman Place apartment and hops and skips from location to location to keep pace with the magnificent Auntie Mame. Director Bob Buseick would have liked to present each scene and location realistically, but he thought it would have created theatrical havoc backstage and brought instantaneous bankruptcy to any theater. He had faith that the imagination of the audience would supply the incidental backgrounds, for the play is the thing—not the settings. At the time, this was the first local production in a single setting. The simple changes that were made throughout the 23 scenes were accomplished by two property staffers, Edward Gross and Margret Fielding. The seating at the old Methodist church was inadequate. During the highly successful run of *Auntie Mame* in the 1964–1965 season, the receipts from one performance were earmarked to start the "Chair Fund," and a total of $368 was set aside. Various garden clubs and civic and church groups also backed the fund. In 1965, Portland Civic Auditorium accepted a bid by Lake Oswego Community Theatre to purchase 124 upholstered chairs at a cost of $3.50 per chair. Volunteers dismantled the chairs at Portland Civic Auditorium and brought them to Lake Oswego Community Theatre.

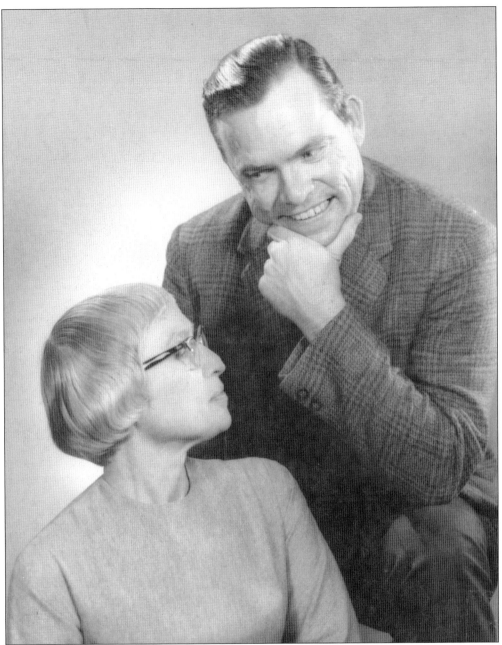

THE MOUSETRAP. Agatha Christie's *The Mousetrap*, known as "the world's longest-running play," has been running since 1952 and shares an anniversary with Lakewood Theatre Company. The play is not about the crime—it is about the solving of the crime. Eight strangers are stranded by a snowstorm and trapped in a guest house. A murderer is among them—but who? Everyone has secrets, and no one is what they seem. In 1965, the Lake Oswego Community Theatre production was directed by Jack Lee Powell, the drama director at Lake Oswego High School. Margaret Pittman (left), an English professor at Lake Oswego High School, played Mrs. Boyle, an unpleasant woman who is highly critical. John B. Moore (right) played Mr. Paravicini. Unfortunately, Mrs. Boyle becomes one of the victims at the Monkswell Manor.

PRIVATE LIVES. From left to right are Hilda Jackson (as Amanda Prynne), Don Youatt (as Elyot Chase), Jim Gray (as Victor Prynne), and Trisha DuBay (as Sybil Chase), formerly Patti Piper. Arlene Gryle (as Louise; not shown) was the assistant to the director in *Private Lives*. The 1965 Lake Oswego Community Theatre production of Noël Coward's *Private Lives* was directed by R. Douglass Peterson, who appeared in many Coward productions and had worked in the drama department at the University of Puget Sound. This romantic comedy is about a lovely summer evening in France turning upside down when a divorced couple unexpectedly honeymoons at the same place with their new spouses.

THE FANTASTICKS. From left to right are (first row, seated on the floor) Garry Rieg (as The Mute); (second row) David Gauch (as Henry), Raymond House (as Mortimer), Ron Jongeward (as Bellamy), and Robert MacLean (as El Gallo); (third row) Bruce Emmons (as Hucklebee), Linda Davis (as Luisa), and Mike Pippi (as Matt). Lake Oswego Community Theatre's third musical was *The Fantasticks*, produced by the group in 1965. Two fathers both think their mediocre offspring are "fantastic." The fathers devise a plan to trick the girl and boy into believing they are involved in an abduction, and by doing so, they will become romantically linked. The couple is mortified to learn that the abduction was staged. Eventually, the couple realizes that they are in love. This production was directed, choreographed, and designed by Jim Erickson.

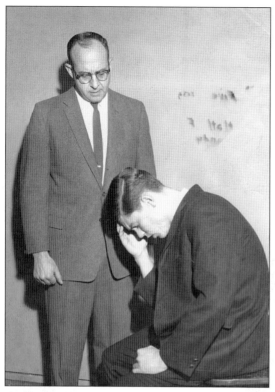

FIVE FINGER EXERCISE. In 1966, Mike Booth (left; as Stanley Harrington, self-made businessman and husband of Louise) and Bob Simpkins (right; as Clive, son of Louise) performed in *Five Finger Exercise*, directed by David Spooner. Clive resists his father's attempt to bond with him as Stanley continues to berate the young man for being too "sensitive." Both parents use Clive as a weapon against one another. When a tutor is plunged into the shouting family drama, Louise finds herself becoming romantically drawn to the tutor, Walter. Meanwhile, Clive develops a crush on Walter as well. *Five Finger Exercise* is a bold psychological drama that invited conversation around repressed homosexuality, human desires, and family conflict.

LITTLE MARY SUNSHINE. In 1966, Connie Peterson (right) played Mary "Little Mary Sunshine" Potts, and Joe Berglund (left) played Cpl. "Billy" Jester. This was an original show written especially for presentation in a small theater. Little Mary Sunshine, foster daughter of Chief Brown Bear of the Kadota tribe, is being threatened by the federal government to foreclose on her Colorado Inn, which is located on disputed land. The courts eventually uphold Chief Brown Bear's claim to the land, which represents one-fourth of Colorado. The chief gives Mary the inn's land and dedicates the rest for a national park—a place the Rangers can call home. In the finale, a miraculously reformed Yellow Feather reappears, waving a large American flag. Several couples seem headed for the altar. Jim Erickson, who directed the musical for Lake Oswego Community Theatre, gestured so strongly at the cast during a rehearsal that he accidentally poked a finger into an eye and cut his eyeball. After being treated at Good Samaritan Hospital, he spent some time in bed with bandages. All turned out well for all involved.

THE MOON IS BLUE. From left to right are James Gray (as Donald Gresham), Tyler Marshall (as Slater), and Dee Weisenborn Young (as Patty O'Neill). In June 1966, the Lake Oswego Community Theatre opened *The Moon Is Blue*. The story begins with the meeting of two New Yorkers, Donald Gresham and Patty O'Neill. Don invites Patty over to his apartment for a drink, and she accepts. Slater, the neighbor, stops by and is also interested in seducing Patty. Patty calls herself a "virgin." At the time, it was a controversial romantic comedy about male and female relationships that uphold the sanctity of marriage—or not. Slater admittedly had "no principles whatsoever."

TINY ALICE. From left to right are Lawrence McKinney (as Cardinal), Roald B. Wulff (as Julian), James Cranna (as Butler), Janet Penner (as Miss Alice), and Mike Booth (as Lawyer). In 1966, Lake Oswego Community Theatre director Del F. Corbett was a drama teacher at Parkrose Senior High School. The library of the castle was constructed by James Peterson. *Tiny Alice*, written by Edward Albee, is a three-act play that mixes religion and corruption. The lawyer offers the cardinal $100 million a year at the request of Miss Alice, the world's richest woman. Julian, the cardinal's secretary, is to come to Miss Alice's castle to complete the details, but while there, Julian falls prey to Miss Alice's seductive ways. Below, Julian is comforted by Miss Alice after suffering from a gunshot wound inflicted by the lawyer.

Luv. Diana Dell Minor (left) and Mike Booth are pictured at left. Directed by Bob Buseick in 1967, *Luv* is an adult comedy by Murray Schisgal and a wildly funny spoof on avant-garde drama featuring a triangle of people matched in misery. Minor had performed in 27 shows and directed several productions at this point. Booth was a member of the Lake Oswego Community Theatre board of directors and helped remodel the theater's basement.

Luv Playbill. This 1967 playbill was printed and designed by June Ellis, Jean Scott, Betty Dent, and Margaret Fielding; the cover artist is unknown. This 14-page playbill was not only informational but also an invitation. Although the theater was governed by a board of directors, the playbill states that "enthusiasm is the only prerequisite for participation." It included the theater's history and highlights; future show information; a cast list; cast biographies; staff acknowledgments; information about children's theater, classes, workshops, play readings, and informal gatherings; and—of course—advertisements.

SLOW DANCE ON THE KILLING GROUND. In the above photograph, from left to right are Jim Phillips (as Randy, also known as "Hip"), Roy Setziol (as Glas), and Linda Davis (as Rosie). In November 1967, Lake Oswego Community Theatre opened *Slow Dance on the Killing Ground.* The three characters' lives converge, each with their own feelings of frustration and loneliness, in this psychological drama. Roald B. Wulff, the director of the LOCT production, was a teacher of speech and theater at Clark College in Vancouver. Born in Paris, Arkansas, Phillips attended Roosevelt High School. He was active in the Portland theater scene at the New Theatre and Portland Civic Theatre.

BURNING OF THE MORTGAGE. From left to right are (first row, kneeling/squatting) Matt Finnigan and Mike Booth; (second row, standing) Jack Lee Powell, Margaret Pittman, Connie Peterson, Betty Dent, Cynthia Watkins, Ken Saddler, Betty Knox, and June Ellis. In 1961, Lake Oswego Community Theatre signed the mortgage agreement for the church building located at 156 Greenwood Road. Then, in June 1967, the burning of the mortgage took place at the home of Betty and Al Knox during the group's annual meeting amid cheers and bravos from the crowd. In fact, the board received a standing ovation. Lake Oswego Community Theatre performed 110 productions over 18 years in the church building. The space was designated as a historical building by the Oswego Heritage Council in 1970 and is now a private residence.

A FUNNY THING HAPPENED ON THE WAY TO THE FORUM. This lively musical production opened on April 20, 1968, directed by Jim Erickson. From left to right are (first row) Martin Brother (The Protean), Diana Dell Minor (Domina), and Robert MacLean (Senex); (second row) Joan Quinton-Cox (Panacea), Charles Bourret (Hysterium), Jerry Halsey (Hero), Joy Marshall (Philia), and Louann Evans (Tintinabula); (third row) Colleen Brown (Vibrata), George Puterbaugh (Lycus), Sally Ford (née Puterbaugh) (Gynmnasia), and Jack Shields (Pseudolus); (fourth row) Scott Sheffield (The Protean), Rich Frishholz (The Protean), Marjorie Post (The Geminae), Don Finlay (Miles Gloriosus), and Jann Mersereau (The Geminae), The story begins 200 years before the Christian era in Rome in front the homes of Erronius, Senex, and Lycus. Besides the singing and movement, one critical piece of this play is comedy. Jack Shields played Psuedolus, a slave with a crafty wit. Senex was the slave master, and fellow slave Hysterium provided plenty of comedic support. Miles Gloriosus stood out as a ridiculously arrogant soldier.

COME BLOW YOUR HORN. In 1968, Betty Knox was the producer and Dr. William Iron was the director of the Neil Simon comedy *Come Blow Your Horn*. Suzanne Price (right) played the role of Peggy, and Ron Miller (left) played the part of Alan. Alan is a confirmed bachelor living in New York City, and his brother comes to stay with him. Smooth-talking Alan wants to help his brother woo a beautiful neighbor named Peggy. Price is the granddaughter of Mr. and Mrs. George Rogers, a Lake Oswego pioneer family. George Rogers Park is adjacent to Lakewood Center for the Arts. George Rogers's home is located in the heart of Old Town, one of Oswego's earliest neighborhoods, which was created primarily for workers of the Oregon Iron and Steel Company. The Rogers home was added to the National Register of Historic Places in 1996.

WHITE LIARS AND BLACK COMEDY. In February 1969, *White Liars* and *Black Comedy*, two very different one-act plays, were performed at Lake Oswego Community Theatre. Portland actress Margaret Barney played a medium as Sophie, Baroness Lemberg, in *White Liars*. From her run-down seaside resort in England, Sophie tells fortunes to Tom (at left in the above image; played by Len Elwell) and Frank (at right in the above image; played by Bill Bower). *Black Comedy* begins in the dark with an unusual production twist. From the conversation on stage, the actors seem to not notice that it is dark. When the stage lights come on, the actors react to a fuse that has blown out and are in complete darkness. Below are Joe Berglund (as Brindsley Miller) and Susan Davis (as Miss Furnival).

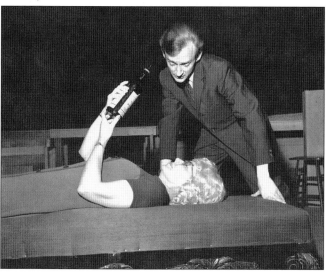

CAST OF BLACK COMEDY. From left to right are Susan Davis (as Miss Furnival), Sally Puterbaugh (as Carol Melkett), Joe Berglund (as Brindsley Miller), Harvey Giffin (as Harold Gorringe), Suzanne Price (as Clea), Roy Schreiber (as Schuppanzigh), Fred Jessey (as Georg Bamberger) and George Puterbaugh (as Colonel Melkett). Dr. William Iron directed the cast to move in the supposed darkness on set. The couple, Brindsley and Carol, stole furniture from their neighbor Harold to impress Carol's father, Colonel Melkett, and Georg, a wealthy art collector. When Harold returns, the chaos begins. Brindsley and Carol keep their guests in the dark—both figuratively and literally. Brindsley's mistress Clea stops by unannounced, and when Carol finds out about the affair, she breaks off her engagement toe Brindsley. Miss Furnival is a spinster who gets drunk by mixing and pouring various drinks. Colonel Melkett is an aloof father who does not seem to be bothered by the craziness that surrounds him.

The Urchins. In April 1969, the Urchins in *The Roar of the Greasepaint—The Smell of the Crowd* were played by, from left to right, (first row) Jan Lingren, Penny Merritt, and Judith Tucker; (second row) Markie Post, Wendy Dustin, Margo Waldron, and Terry Kepert. Post, the famous actress from *Night Court*, got her start at Lake Oswego Community Theatre and Lewis & Clark College.

The Roar of the Greasepaint—The Smell of the Crowd. This show is the story of the game of life like a Laurel and Hardy situation set to music. The play, created by Anthony Newley and Leslie Bricusse, was directed and choreographed by Jim Erickson for the Lake Oswego Community Theatre production. Pictured here are, from left to right, Martin Brother (Cocky), Pat Clopper (The Kid), Jim Phillips (The Negro), Jack Shields (Sir), and Julie Kirkpatrick (The Girl). George Puterbaugh (not shown) played The Bully. Phillips played this same role in a Portland Civic Theatre production, raising his voice in the rich musical exclamation of "Feeling Good."

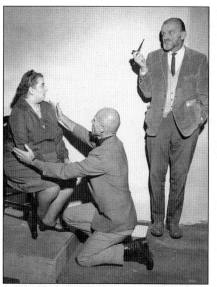

HALFWAY UP THE TREE. From left to right are Sandi Gardner (as Lady Fitzbuttress), George Puterbaugh (as Tiny Gilliatt-Brown), and Vince Panny (as General Sir Mallalieu Fitzbuttress). Dr. William Iron of Lewis & Clark College directed this production in 1969; he was also the founder of the Lewis & Clark Summer Tent Theatre. The assistant director was Sally Puterbaugh, who acted in several Lake Oswego Community Theatre productions, including *The Roar of the Greasepaint—The Smell of the Crowd*.

GENERATION GAP. From left to right are Rick Johnson (as Robert), George Puterbaugh (as Tiny Gilliatt-Brown), Sherrie Iron (as Judy), and Sandi Gardner (as Lady Fitzbuttress). Lady Fitzbuttress thinks that maybe a sword will bridge the generation gap. Peter Ustinov's *Halfway Up the Tree* is a comedy about a British family beset with misunderstandings of the generation gap. The son of George and Sally Puterbaugh, Cliff, recently returned to Lakewood Theatre Company to sell smoked jerky at a "Whiskey on Wednesday" night.

SILENT NIGHT, LONELY NIGHT. In November 1969, Lake Oswego Community Theatre presented this drama in two acts written by Robert Anderson. Pictured at right are Rick Rease as Jerry and Barbara Lane (née Chatas) as Katherine. The story is set at a Colonial Inn in a New England town on Christmas Eve. Katherine frets about an unfaithful husband and picking up her son Jerry from a nearby prep school. Then she meets John, a married man with his wife staying in a sanitarium. They find consolation and sleep together before returning to their old lives. Rease was a student at Our Lady of the Lake and performed in plays at the school and at Portland Civic Theatre. Barbara Lane wrote copy and did production work for promotional spots at KGW. A few weeks before the play opened, Al Laue (pictured below as John) was appointed to be the assistant attorney general for the State of Oregon.

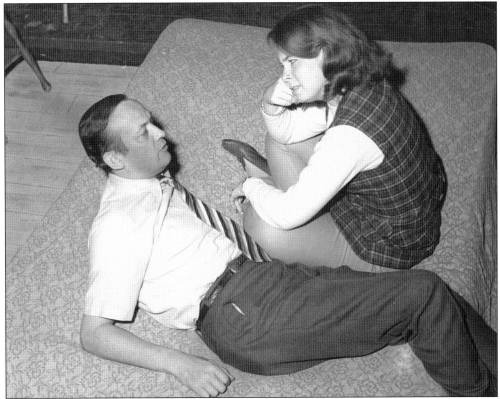

A STREETCAR NAMED DESIRE.
Kathy King (right) played the
role of Stella, and Tony Giordano
(left) played Stanley. In 1972,
this production won "Best
Director" (Philip Bonfiglio),
"Best Actor" (Tony Giordano),
"Best Actress" (Delight Lorenz),
"Best Supporting Actor" (Mike
Booth), and "Best Play" at the
first Oregon Theatrical Awards
Society (OTAS) awards.

**PIXIE RUMBOLZ IN THE
PAJAMA GAME.** In this April
1972 production, the role of
Gladys was played by Pixie
Rumbolz, who had been active
in Portland Civic Theater and
Slabtown productions. She
served as chairman of "Theater
Wing," which sponsors acting
classes and promotes theater
involvement. Rumbolz won
"Best Supporting Actress" at the
first Oregon Theatrical Awards
Society (OTAS) awards for her
role in *The Pajama Game.*

CABARET. In 1973, this group of lovelies welcomed audiences to Lake Oswego Community Theatre's production of *Cabaret*, produced by Karen and Jim Conway. The musical is based on *I Am a Camera*, a play written by John Van Druten and set in 1931 Berlin nightlife. Above, from left to right are Jeanni LaTourette, Maggie Marmaduke, Kris Peterson, Terry LaTourette, Lisa Dworkin, and Cynthia Petersen. Below, director Ken Lewis helps Bob Nielsen apply makeup for a rehearsal. Nielsen played the Emcee of the Kit Kat Club. In the 1972–1973 season, *Cabaret* won several categories in the Oregon Theatrical Awards Society (OTAS) awards. The LOCT member voters chose Leslie Denniston (who played Sally Bowles) as "Best Actress," Nielsen as "Best Supporting Actor," Lewis as "Best Director," and *Cabaret* as the "Best Play."

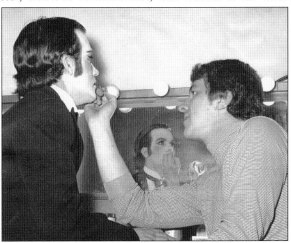

Lake Oswego Community Theatre

156 Greenwood Rd., Lake Oswego, Ore.
636-9061

FEIFFER'S PEOPLE

Adults $3.50   Students $2.50

FEIFFER'S PEOPLE. Lake Oswego Community Theatre presented *Feiffer's People* in November 1973. The admission ticket shows the price for one adult at $3.50, and $2.50 for a student. This audience was in for a different kind of performance—a sketch comedy. The show was originally based on a series of comic strips by Jules Feiffer. This allowed the actors the freedom to portray different roles.

CAST OF FEIFFER'S PEOPLE. This contemporary musical revue was written by Jules Feiffer, and the Lake Oswego Community Theatre production was directed by Richard Hurst and John Zagone. From left to right are (first row) Barbara Low and Chrisse Roccaro; (second row) Monte Merrick, Leslie Denniston, Maureen Lind, Joan Denk, and Bob Trudo; (third row) Zagone (musical director), Steve Knox (no relation to executive producer Steve Knox), Bill Deane, and Hurst. Without a singular plotline, the play was a challenge for the cast and exciting for the audience with its constant character and scene changes.

GODSPELL. In 1974, the Lake Oswego Community Theatre presented *Godspell.* From left to right are Lisa Knox (née Olsen), Michael Schauerman (as Jesus; standing behind Knox), David Itkin, and Dorene Horn. It was directed by Richard Hurst, the musical director was Vera Long, and the set and lighting design was by Peter West. It was produced by Kay Griffin Vega. *Godspell* is a musical based upon the Gospel according to St. Matthew.

OLIVER. In the fall of 1974, Rick Porterfield, a singing sixth-grader from Fernwood School, played Oliver Twist. Directed and choreographed by Vicky Vose, this play is adapted from Charles Dickens's novel *Oliver Twist*, the story of a 19th-century orphan and his experiences in London. Behind the scenes, the six-member orchestra was directed by Patricia Reich.

GEORGE M! This poster was designed by Kevin Lindsey to promote the 1974 Lake Oswego Community Theatre production of *George M!*. It was a family affair for director and choreographer Millie Hoelscher—her daughter Gretchen appeared as First Little Girl, and her husband, Bill, built the set.

CAST OF GEORGE M! The cast of *George M!* took the stage during Lake Oswego Community Theatre's 22nd season in April 1974. From left to right are (first row) Bill Morris (as Sam Harris) and Nancy Quinn Faunt (as Fay Templeton); (second row) Paul Yarnell (as E.F. Albee), John Lewis (as Director), Dave Lane (as Hank), Rick Livingston (as Walt), and Brian Albro (as Louis Behman). *George M!* is based on the life of Broadway star George M. Cohan.

O.T.A.S. AWARD WINNERS

BEST ACTOR **71/72** BEST ACTRESS — TONY GIORDANO / DELIGHT LORENZ

BEST ACTOR **72/73** BEST ACTRESS — STEVE KNOX / LESLIE DENNISTON

BEST SUPPORTING ACTOR / BEST SUPPORTING ACTRESS — MIKE BOOTH / PIXIE RUMBOLZ

BEST SUPPORTING ACTRESS / BEST SUPPORTING ACTOR — DEANNE PIERCEY / BOB NIELSEN

BEST ACTOR **73/74** BEST ACTRESS — MORRIE DRAGOON / ELLYN ANDERSON

BEST SUPPORTING ACTOR / BEST SUPPORTING ACTRESS — FRANK WAPLES / VICKI VOSE

Lake Oswego

Community Theatre

Needs your membership and support - Join Now!

*Receive Drama Card Discount
*Be eligible to vote in this season's Oregon Theatrical Awards Society selections
*Receive our newsletter

Dues are:
$5.00 family
$2.50 solo

You may join at the box office—ticket office—or by mail. P.O. Box 274, Lake Oswego, 97034

OREGON THEATRICAL AWARDS SOCIETY. Lake Oswego Community Theatre's OTAS award winners were included inside the playbill for the 1974 production of *George M!* Presented annually since the 1971–1972 season, the awards recognize extraordinary performances and artistic and technical talent. *A Streetcar Named Desire* won almost every category in 1972, including "Best Actor," "Best Actress," "Best Supporting Actor," "Best Play," and "Best Director." "Best Supporting Actress" went to Pixie Rumbolz for her work in *The Pajama Game*. In 1972–1973, "Best Actor" was awarded to Steve Knox for *Butterflies Are Free*. Leslie Denniston won "Best Actress" for her performance in *Cabaret*. "Best Supporting Actor" went to Bob Nielsen for *Cabaret*. "Best Supporting Actress" was Deanne Piercy for *Butterflies Are Free*. In 1973–1974, "Best Actor" went to Morrie Dragoon for *Man of La Mancha*. Ellyn Anderson won "Best Actress" for *Wait Until Dark*. The winners of "Best Supporting Actor" and "Best Supporting Actress" went to Frank Waples and Vickie Vose, respectively, for their performances in *Anything Goes*. Currently, OTAS has 18 categories plus additional awards, including the Betty Kingsbury Heritage Award for exemplary service to the theater. All Lakewood Theatre Company members may cast a ballot for the awards.

65

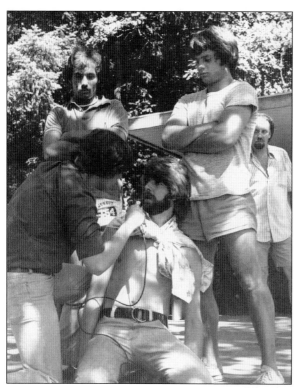

JESUS CHRIST SUPERSTAR. On August 21, 1975, Lake Oswego Community Theatre opened the rock musical *Jesus Christ Superstar*. The story is about the last seven days in the life of Jesus of Nazareth as interpreted via music composed by Andrew Lloyd Webber with lyrics by Tim Rice. In the image at left, John Lewis (as Pilate) holds the microphone as Kerry Sensenbach (as Jesus) kneels. Behind Lewis and Sensenbach are Ed Polich (left), Bob Polich (center), and Arnold Sterling. The first four performances were held outdoors at the Riverdale School. Seating was provided on bleachers or on the ground. Audience members were encouraged to bring blankets and cushions. *Jesus Christ Superstar* reopened for indoor performances on September 4, 1975. Below are Kurt Misar (as Peter) and Lisa Knox (née Olsen; as Mary), who performed to multiple sold-out houses.

SOLD-OUT SHOWS. Indoor performances were held at the old Methodist church at 156 Greenwood Road. It only held about 100 people, so reservations were a must. Because of the unusually high demand for tickets, *Jesus Christ Superstar* was held over and played at Lakeridge High School for an additional weekend. Below, Steve Knox (left), who directed the 35-member cast, talks with Dirk Hillyer, the musical director, in front of the old church building. Knox directed the Lilliput Players children's theater troupe and taught creative dramatics to students at Lake Oswego Community Theatre under the auspices of Portland Community College. He directed his current wife, Lisa Knox (née Olsen), in this memorable production. At the 1975–1976 Oregon Theatrical Awards Society awards, Steve Knox earned the honor of "Best Director" and Hillyer was named "Best Musical Director" for their work on *Jesus Christ Superstar.*

JESUS CHRIST SUPERSTAR ORCHESTRA. Above are, from left to right, (first row) Pat Reich (on piano), Ann Parson and Kathy Martin (on flute), and Laire Halling (on the clarinet); (second row) Steve Watkins, Bonnie Kovaleff, and Todd Nelson (on trumpet), and Chuck Dieter (on trombone). Below are, from left to right, Ralph Cunningham (on bass), Dave Bennett (on guitar), and Tom Walpole (on drums), with musical director Dirk Hillyer playing keyboard (he also played the French horn). The contemporary rock opera was performed by this live orchestra. Ralph Cunningham, the sound technician, established a balance between the vocalists and instruments.

STEVE KNOX AS CHARLEY'S AUNT. In 1976, Lake Oswego Community Theatre staged *Charley's Aunt*, a hilarious farce. Steve Knox (at right in the above image) starred as Lord Fancourt Babberley (dressed as Charley's aunt), and John Lewis (at left in the above image) played Stephen Spettigue, an earnest solicitor and aggressive suitor of the faux aunt. Knox gave a strong portrayal of Charley's well-to-do aunt from Brazil, hurdling over furniture and fending off money-grubbing machismo. He noted playing Lord Fancourt Babberley as "seeking perfection in my art, and realizing that comedy borders on making an ass of oneself; my goal is to make a perfect ass of myself." Below are Knox (left) and Kurt Misar (as Charley Wykeham).

CHARLEY'S AUNT. In the image at left, from left to right are Nicci Cooke (as Kitty Verdun), Kurt Misar (as Charley Wykeham), and Marie Hahn (as Amy Spettigue) in Lake Oswego Community Theatre's 1976 production of *Charley's Aunt*. Kitty is loved by Jack Chesney and a dear friend of Amy. Amy loves Charley Wykeham. Jack, a friend of Kurt, contrives to have Lord Babberley pose as Charley's aunt in order to induce a couple of pretty girls, Kitty and Amy, to meet at his house for dinner. Below are Michael Walling (left), who played Jack Chesney, and Steve Knox, who played Lord Fancourt Babberley/Charley's aunt.

COUNT DRACULA. In 1976, Leslie Sarnoff directed *Count Dracula*, based on Bram Stoker's 19th-century novel, *Dracula*. Sarnoff served as a morning DJ on Portland's KINK radio station for 22 years. This play is a witty version of the classic story of a suave vampire whose passion is sinking his teeth into the throats of beautiful young women. John McComb (standing in the image at right) played Count Dracula, with Kay Pollack as Mina (seated), and Greg Capshaw as Jonathan Hacker. The comedy was directed by Leslie Sarnoff. Below are Count Dracula and his latest victim, Mina.

CAST OF COUNT DRACULA. The cast of *Count Dracula* included Kay Pollack as Mina (seated); Jim Shultze as Renfield (directly behind Pollack); and, from left to right (standing), Bob Brooks as Hennessey (left), Dale Alan Cooke as Dr. Arthur Seward, Ann Olsen as Sybil Seward, Jon McComb as Count Dracula, Greg Capshaw as Jonathan Harker, Leslie Sarnoff as Heinrich Van Helsing, and Barry Cripe as Wesley. Offstage, McComb was a DJ at KYXI. His radio voice worked well for his role as Count Dracula. This was an exciting show with many special effects. Count Dracula could transform himself into a bat, materialize from fog, and dissolve into mist. Bats flew over the audience. Olsen, who played Sybil, the sherry-sipping sister and the asylum's lush, won rounds of applause. The show opened on February 27, 1976, at Lake Oswego Community Theatre.

SWEET CHARITY. Above, from left to right are Anne Mangan (as Betsy), Kathi McKern (as Chorus), Stephanie Davison (as Helene), Marta Mellinger (as Nickie), Lori Marnon (as Charity), Michelle Gray (as Rosie), and Dianne McDougall (as Ursala). In April 1976, Lake Oswego Community Theatre opened *Sweet Charity*, directed by Richard Hurst with musical direction by Vera Long. Charity is a dance hostess who falls in love easily and often. In real life, Marnon is a former Las Vegas showgirl who performed in *Folies Bergere* at Tropicana and *Minsky's Burlesque* at the Aladdin. Below, the cast is shown singing "Rhythm of Life." From left to right are (first row) Charisse Rumbolz and Trudi Merwin; (second row) Davison and Mangan; (third row) John Allen, Kerry Sensenbach, Andrew Edwards (playing Big Daddy under the pseudonym George Spelvin), Clifford Bell, and David Lane; (fourth row) Larry LaFreniere, McDougall, Michael Walling, Marnon, Gray, and Clifton Swinford; (fifth row) McKern, Jeff Ekdahl, Mellinger, and Tony Giordano.

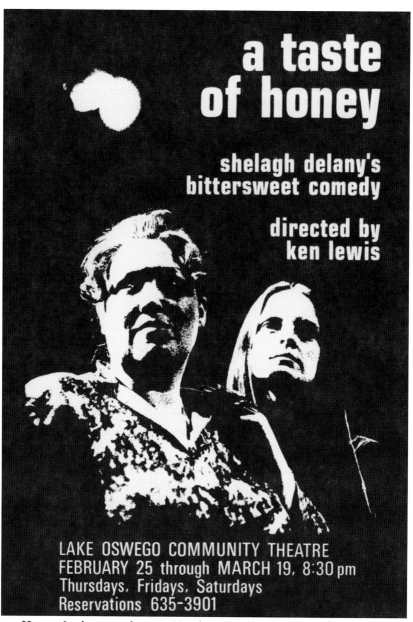

a taste of honey

shelagh delany's
bittersweet comedy

directed by
ken lewis

LAKE OSWEGO COMMUNITY THEATRE
FEBRUARY 25 through MARCH 19, 8:30 pm
Thursdays, Fridays, Saturdays
Reservations 635-3901

A TASTE OF HONEY. In this comedy set in Northwest England in the 1950s, Jo (played by Cyndy Collver) is a 17-year-old when her overbearing, self-serving mother Helen (played by Gail Slocum) leaves home to be with her lover. The Boy, a black sailor (played by Benjamin Jacobs) begins a relationship with Jo. The boy proposes marriage to Jo, then goes to sea. Jo is left pregnant and alone. Geoffrey (played by Michael Walling) assumes the role as a surrogate father. The play is a truthful and tragic portrayal of life with class, race, gender and sexual orientation all rolled into one. In 1977, the theater had 100 seats and sold tickets for $4 for general admission and $3.50 for students and seniors. Lake Oswego Community Theatre held 11 performances of *A Taste of Honey* from February 25 through March 19, 1977. The sold-out crowds laughed, cried, and fantasized. The play, written by Shelagh Delaney, was the first work of an 18-year-old who had left school at age 16, tried her hand at various jobs, and then wrote this bittersweet comedy.

Irma la Douce. In September 1977, the sexy and saucy *Irma La Douce* opened at Lake Oswego Community Theatre, directed/choreographed by Millie Hoelscher with musical direction by Larry Cunningham. Playing to sold-out houses, the frolicking French romp was led by Pat Brown Clopper (at left in the image at right) as Irma La Douce and Kirby Griffin (right), who played the dual role of Nestor Le Fripe and Monsieur Oscar. Nestor, down on his luck, goes to the French café/music hall of Chez Moustache, a popular hangout for prostitutes and pimps. After saving Irma from her abusive pimp, Nestor moves in with her and unwittingly becomes Irma's new pimp. It is a clever play chock full of satire and commentary on human existence.

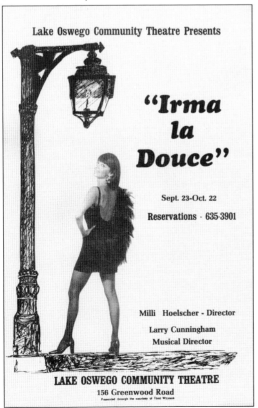

Lake Oswego Community Theatre Presents

"Irma la Douce"

Sept. 23-Oct. 22

Reservations · 635-3901

Milli Hoelscher - Director

Larry Cunningham
Musical Director

LAKE OSWEGO COMMUNITY THEATRE
156 Greenwood Road

Presented through the courtesy of Toni Wizman

CHICAGO. Pictured here are Pat Piltz (as the Matron) and Penny Stephens (as Roxie Hart). To kick off the Lake Oswego Community Theatre's 1980–1981 season, the vaudeville musical *Chicago*, based on the play *Chicago* by Maurine Dallas Watkins, was presented in September 1980. It was directed by Paul Douroumis, a school director at Portland Civic Theatre. The executive producer, Kay Griffin Vega, had only a few hours to replace a cast member who was hospitalized with a kidney stone, but who would come in and sing "All That Jazz" and "Razzle Dazzle" at the last minute? Vega called theater manager (now executive director) Andrew Edwards to fill in, even though he did not know a single line in the musical. The crowd of 200 was informed of the emergency. Edwards arrived at the theater with 15 minutes to spare. He stepped on stage with script in hand and did not disappoint.

CAST OF *THE PAJAMA GAME.* From left to right are (first row) Gary Reynolds (as Sid Sorokin) and Pam Spradin (as Babe Williams); (second row) Katrina Van der Horst (as Gladys), Andrew Edwards (as Hines), Paul B. Bender (as Hasler), B. Gail Hillyer (as Mabel), and Larry Bozarth (as Prez). Babe, the chairwoman of the union grievance committee, hopes to force her boss (Sid Sorokin) to raise the workers' minimum wage by 7.5¢ to about 67¢ an hour.

THE PAJAMA GAME. Babe Williams (played by Pam Spradin) is unsure of Hines's knife-throwing ability. Hines (played by Andrew Edwards) is the timekeeper at Sleep-Tite Pajama Factory. The assembly line speeds up to hilarity in this tuneful look at the eternal battle between management and labor. From May 9 through June 14, 1980, Lake Oswego Community Theatre presented *The Pajama Game* at the 156 Greenwood Road location.

No, No, Nanette. From left to right are Mary Lewis, Sioban Charlesworth, Kay Griffin Vega, Diana Duncan, and Susan Ruddock. Vega played Sue in *No, No, Nanette* in 1986. As executive producer of Lake Oswego Community Theatre, Vega oversaw all productions and educational programs. It was her job to select the shows for each season. She said, "it has to have a good story that is entertaining, and also I want the audience to learn something." Vega would often travel to other cities to see shows as a way of determining whether a specific show would appeal to Lakewood audiences. In partnership with Breakaway Tours, Kay started a theater tour that regularly travels to New York City and London to see shows and visit local sites.

Three

LAKEWOOD SCHOOL BECOMES LAKEWOOD CENTER FOR THE ARTS

LAKEWOOD SCHOOL. This building, located at 368 S. State Street, sits on the former site of Oswego Grammar School. Lakewood School was designed by Luther Lee Dougan and opened on September 17, 1928. The school closed in 1980, at which point it was turned over to the Lake Oswego Community Theatre by the school board chairman, Jerry Isom, for the purpose of converting the school into the Lakewood Center for the Arts. (Courtesy of Lake Oswego Library.)

LAKEWOOD SCHOOL STATE STREET ENTRANCE. The Lakewood School sits on land originally owned by Albert Alonzo Durham as part of his 640-acre donation land claim. Early development revolved around the Old Town neighborhood, where the Durhams built their home. Built in 1928, the structure has many features of Classical Revival architecture from between 1895 and 1950. These features include formal symmetrical design with prominent center entrances, porticos with full-height columns, decorative doors, and rectangular double-hung windows. The Lakewood School also features quoins, plaster festoons, relief medallions of George Washington and Abraham Lincoln, and a belvedere that corresponds with Georgian and Federal styles. (Author's collection.)

DAY JOB. The Girod family moved from Baker, Oregon, with two young boys and lived across from Lakewood School in a small home. Stan Girod started as a fifth-grade teacher and later served as a vice principal and principal of Lakewood School. The above photograph shows Stan Girod's sixth-grade class in 1955 at Lakewood School. A man of many talents, Girod is shown at right playing Luther Billis in Lake Oswego Community Theatre's production of *South Pacific* in 1963. Luther, dressed as Honey Bun in a blond wig, grass skirt, and coconut-shell bra, has little to no respect for authority and is always scheming. Girod provided much-needed comic relief for his fellow sailors in the play and for students in the classroom. (Above, courtesy of Lake Oswego Library.)

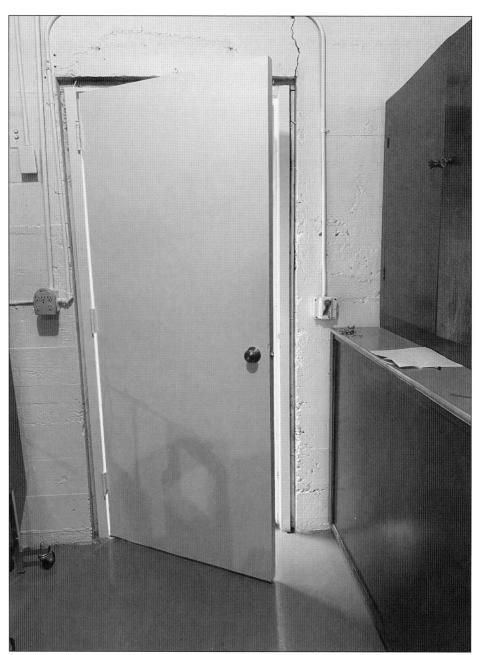

BOILER ROOM HAUNTING. If a trip to the principal's office was not enough to correct a student's behavior, the unlucky student might be sent to the boiler room. The boiler was a huge clunky device with oily smells and creaky sounds located in the dimly lit basement without windows. Inside the boiler room, the misbehaving student may have been given a swift whack from a paddle. The few students who could attest to having been inside the boiler room claimed it had haunting sounds. The noises scared them, and some say they saw a "glow." These students became folk heroes in the classroom. Some staff members have seen things move around or heard unfamiliar noises in the room. Although the claims are unproven, the legend of the creepy boiler room continues to chill to the bone. (Author's collection.)

GRADUATION CLASS. In 1947, these eighth-grade graduates stood in front of Lakewood School. From left to right are (first row) Diane Spencer, Jack Day, Dale Jones, Bob Munger, Kirq Shanks, Jerry Giesy, Eddie VanPelt, Richard Phillips, Charles Whitmore, and Jay Flood; (second row) Jackie Steaurt, Dorcas Waldorf, Shirley Ryan, Janet Gardner, Vera Chapman, Ann Grover, Edna Kirk, Mary Lou Perry, and Dolores Davis (third row); Janis Carothers, Lee McGary, Judy Brear, Barbara Wolfington, Irene Hawkins, Elizabeth Ekvall, Mary Grossenbacher, and teacher Mr. Little. (Courtesy of Lake Oswego Library.)

LAKEWOOD CLASSROOM AND PLAYGROUND. Above, students listen to Kay Needham in the classroom at Lakewood School in 1945. World events did not go unnoticed by the students who practiced duck-and-cover A-bomb drills. World War II begins to near its end in April 1945. By the end of the month, it was clear that Nazi Germany would fall, and the Allies would only accept unconditional surrender. Fighting continued in the Pacific, and the war with Japan did not end until September, after the United States dropped the first atomic bombs on Japan. A bomb shelter was built close to Lakewood School in the early 1950s by a group of local fathers. It was dug into the hillside that runs along Greenwood Road. The entrance was located diagonally across from the old Methodist church. The shelter had support beams on the top and sides, a gravel floor, and bench-type seats for about 20 people. (Both, courtesy of Lake Oswego Library.)

Snow White at the Circus. From left to right are Lisa Coury (as Snow White), Anna Donner (as the Fortune Teller/Wicked Queen), and LaVerne Springer (as the Ringmaster). They led the cast of mostly child performers in *Snow White at the Circus*, directed by Stan Foote and Sahni Samuelson. This was the first Lake Oswego Community Theatre production held at the new Lakewood Center, located at 368 S. State Street. Below, attendees entertained by *Snow White at the Circus* sat on the Lakewood School gymnasium floor and rented theater risers. The original holiday production of Lakewood's one-ring circus featuring Snow White and the Seven Dwarfs ran from November 29 through December 14, 1980. Over 1,500 people enjoyed the 11 performances of the holiday show.

PRESCHOOL ENGLISH TEA PARTY. Nicole Christianson and Ellyn Anderson opened the Community Arts Preschool in the fall of 1981 at Lakewood Center for the Arts. The school, which served children between the ages of three and five, began with two teachers, one aide, and 32 children. After three years in a single room, the school moved into two rooms and served about 60 children. The school focuses on puppetry, drama, and other arts as ways to prepare children for kindergarten. The partners have found the center an ideal place for their arts preschool. This was also the home of the Lake Oswego Community Theatre and its children's theater, the Collector Gallery, Western Ballet Theatre, Ronda Gates' Danceaerobics, Kay Griffin Vega's piano studio, and the New Lakewood Art Association Gallery. Charles Compton, the owner of the Collector Gallery, invited the preschool to visit the gallery down the hall. In 1983, Christianson took over as director and sole proprietor after Anderson retired.

LAKEWOOD CENTER ASSOCIATES. Above, from left to right are Lakewood Center Associates members Mary Ann Swinford, DeDe Gillespie, Linda Moulton, and Jeannette Johnson. This meeting took place in October 1991. Lakewood Center Associates, an auxiliary arm of the Lakewood Center for the Arts, was formed in 1984. Liz Elston was Lakewood Center Associate's first president. In 1986, the associates assumed the scholarship program that had been coordinated by the Lake Oswego Theatre Guild since 1977. Scholarships are awarded to graduating high school seniors who plan to pursue a career in the performing arts. Various guest speakers, including staff member Betty Brooks (pictured at right), an actress in *Dark Shadows*, are invited to talk to the associates at their monthly luncheons.

RE-RUNS SHOP. Lakewood Center created a space for an art gallery, which is where the resale shop Re-Runs is now located. Workers removed the room's chalk and tack boards and covered the walls with plywood and linen. The coat closet wall was removed. Floodlights, carpeting, movable panels, and a sales counter were added. The Collector Gallery was a private gallery run by Charles Compton in this space. The Lakewood Center Associates relocated Re-Runs from the north end of Lakewood Center to the south end in 1991. This is a photograph of the shop's grand reopening in 1991. Re-Runs is an upscale nonprofit consignment thrift shop managed and staffed by the Lakewood Center Associates of the Lakewood Center for the Arts.

RAVE REVUES COOKBOOK. The Lakewood Center Associates published a cookbook called *Rave Revues* in 1986. The book contained unique recipes from 240 Oregon kitchens and took on a theatrical format (a "playbill" is the menu, "finales" are the desserts.) Former first lady Nancy Reagan signed and submitted her pumpkin pecan pie recipe. Other celebrities submitted recipes, including actress Julianne Phillips, who was married to Bruce "The Boss" Springsteen at Lake Oswego's Our Lady of the Lake Catholic Church. Her recipe was a Roquefort cheese and beer blended rye dip. Sally Struthers, who played Archie Bunker's daughter on the television show *All in the Family*, submitted a recipe for Norwegian butter cookies. The first printing of the book was 3,400 copies, and the second printing was 3,000. The average selling price was $10.65. By March 1990, over 6,000 cookbooks had been sold in the United States and Canada. The books helped fund the paving of the parking lot (at a cost of $7,500) and numerous other projects.

Lakewood Staff. From left to right are (first row) Mary Turnock, Andrew Edwards, Kay Griffin Vega, and Arlene Brice; (second row) Claudette Webster and Betty Brooks; (third row) Ellen Preston, Jackie Culver, Amy Hutson, and Larry Hutson. During the late 1980s, this team played a crucial role in the successful transition from Lake Oswego Community Theatre to Lakewood Theatre Company by launching successful fundraisers, producing more professional shows, increasing theater membership, and offering a variety of programs.

PAL JOEY. In May 1983, *Pal Joey* was the first show to open in the beautiful theater with comfortable new seats, new staging possibilities, and new elegance, making Lakewood Center for the Arts complete. Andrew Edwards directed this 23-person cast of characters, including sleazy cabaret singers, gum-snapping showgirls, and blackmailing gangsters. Joey Evans (played by Martii Campbell), is a charming, unscrupulous opportunist who lands a job as an emcee in a seedy Chicago nightclub in the 1930s. Audiences enjoyed the Rodgers and Hart chorus-line numbers like "Bewitched, Bothered and Bewildered," with musical direction by Sandra Christensen.

ANNIE. The inaugural season at Lakewood Center for the Arts opened with Lake Oswego Community Theatre's production of *Annie* on September 30, 1983. The musical is based on the comic strip *Little Orphan Annie*, which began in New York in 1924 and was created by Harold Gray. Annie (played by Jori Bieze) is left at an orphanage as a baby and then decides at age 11 to try to find her parents and escape the clutches of Miss Hannigan, the orphanage director. When Annie returns to the orphanage, Oliver Warbucks (played by Sunny Sorrels), the billionaire, wants to adopt her. But first, he offers a check to any people who can prove they are Annie's parents. When Miss Hannigan's con artist brother and girlfriend arrive to collect the money, Hannigan joins in on the plot. In the end, all turns out well for Annie and her friends. This production of the play was directed by Millie Hoelscher.

Four

LAKEWOOD THEATRE COMPANY

JOSEPH AND THE AMAZING TECHNICOLOR DREAMCOAT. In 1990, Brooks Ashmanskas (center) played Joseph in the musical *Joseph and the Amazing Technicolor Dreamcoat*. Ashmanskas graduated from Beaverton High School, majored in drama at Bennington College in Vermont, and returned from London's Royal Academy of Dramatic Arts. He has been nominated for multiple Tony Awards, including for his role in *The Prom*. Written by Andrew Lloyd Webber and Tim Rice, the play is inspired by the story of Joseph from the Book of Genesis. Joseph's father gives his son a colorful coat as a token of appreciation, but his 11 brothers are jealous of the generous gift and try to sell Joseph into slavery. This production was directed and choreographed by Jim Erickson and produced by Kay Griffin Vega.

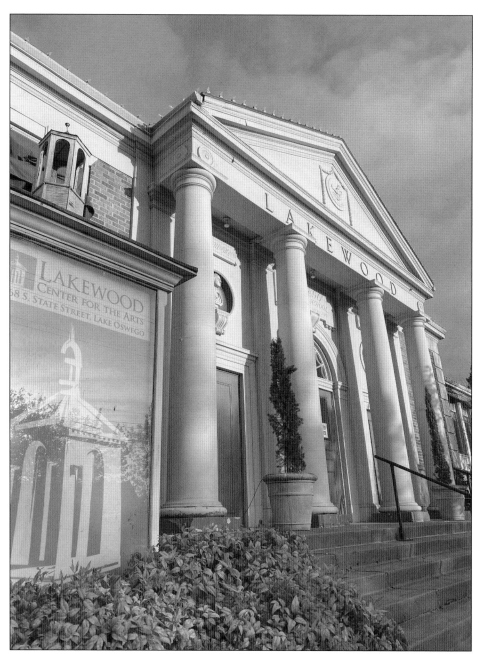

LAKEWOOD THEATRE COMPANY. The Lakewood Theatre Company is the parent nonprofit of Lakewood Center for the Arts. In September 1990, Lake Oswego Community Theatre became Lakewood Theatre Company to more closely identify with all the programs at Lakewood Center and reflect the increasing professionalism and quality of the theater productions. The group's impact on the community as a training ground for emerging artists and performers is expansive. Lakewood Theatre Company presents six productions per year, and its second stage on the lower level, Side Door Stage, produces about four shows annually. By 2012, Lakewood Theatre Company was attracting more than 40,000 people to its shows each year. It is the longest-running nonprofit theater company in the Portland metropolitan area. (Author's collection.)

KAY GRIFFIN VEGA. Since 1972, Vega has been involved in Lake Oswego Community Theatre (LOCT), which later became Lakewood Theatre Company. She served as executive producer, board president, assistant director, actor, singer, dancer, and the person police called when there had been a door left unlocked at LOCT or Lakewood. She hired executive director Andrew Edwards and technical director Kurt Herman, along with countless other staff and production crew members. The LOCT's Oregon Theatrical Awards Society (OTAS) gave Vega (right) the "$100,000 Producer Award" for her work from 1973 to 1979; this award was presented by Michaele Dexter Dunlap. In 1980, Vega was awarded an OTAS as "Best Musical Director" for the show *Something's Afoot*. Lakewood Theatre Company presented Vega with the "Appreciation Award" in 1995, and she was presented with the notable "Lifetime Achievement Award" at the 2010 annual Drammy Awards ceremony, which celebrates outstanding work in Portland-area theater. After she retired in 2016, Vega was named producer emerita of the Lakewood Theatre Company.

GODSPELL IN THE 1990S. In May 1991, Andrew Edwards directed *Godspell* with musical direction by Phil Hilfiker. The cast of *Godspell* included, from left to right, (first row) Ginny Lorts-Grout, Jesse Merz, and Patti Voglino; (second row) Susan Jonsson and Anne De Fresne Gale; (third row) David Rider, Sheryl Birdsell, J.C. Crimp, Joe Costa, and Clif Swinford. The musical features a wide range of folk, rock, and show tunes. The energetic cast dances and sings using the colorful play set, platforms, and slides throughout the performance. The band performed behind a chain-link fence, adding to the playground setting.

ANN OLSEN. In recognition for 30 years of exemplary service, Ann Olsen (left) was presented with the "Betty Kingsbury Heritage Award" by Bill Headlee in 1996. Olsen's first appearance at Lake Oswego Community Theatre was in the role of Stella, the busy reporter, in Jane Erickson's play *The Beloved Rake* in 1960. Olsen played a pivotal role in the organization of the newly formed theater through her roles on the advisory board, as production manager, and working in publicity. She enjoyed a career in writing, acting, and radio production at KIDO in Boise, KIRO in Seattle, and KKEY in Portland. Her first love was always theater. And talent runs in the family—Lisa Knox, one of Olsen's daughters, performed in Lakewood Theatre Company's *Murder on the Nile*, *Young Frankenstein*, and *Sister Act*, among other productions.

BEEHIVE. In the image at left, from left to right are (first row) Linda Brown, Rebecca Kimball, and Debera-Ann Lund; (second row) Stan Foote (director), Cherie Price, and Sue Parks-Hilden. The show opened in August 1996 with Foote serving as director, Karl Mansfield as musical director, and Kay Griffin Vega as producer. The plot of the show spans a decade, from the election of Pres. John F. Kennedy to the first moon shot, and is told through music. Price played Leslie Gore and sang hits like "My Boyfriend's Back," "It's My Party," and "You Don't Own Me." Jeannette Russell Brown (below) sang "Sweet Talkin' Guy" and "Respect."

STAGE HOUSE CONSTRUCTION. The renovation of Lakewood Center for the Arts took an array of talent and years of planning. In 1981, Michaele Dexter Dunlap, design coordinator, laid out a plan to build the new stage house and theater. Local architect Ken Wallin, of Fisher, Wallin & Long, began the design work. The project continued under Harold Long and Steve Poland. People who were on the rigging crews of some of the biggest theaters in New England came to work on the project. The original plan was to build the stage house adjacent to the gymnasium area, which served as the auditorium. In 1982, the board voted to create a 220-seat theater in the gymnasium space instead. After 22 years of planning and fundraising, ground was finally broken on the stage house in 2002.

Stage House Becomes Headlee Mainstage. In 2002, the ground-breaking ceremony for the Lakewood Center stage house took place. The stage house being dedicated to the Headlee family occurred later, on November 6, 2003. The stage house was built in two phases, because Lakewood Theatre Company was only able to close for a one-to-two-month period. In the summer of 2002, the stage house was built with a fly loft system. The flies allowed for extended stage walls, and the scenery could fly up until it was out of sight of the audience. The stage house featured a trapped stage for multistory sets. That summer, Lakewood Theatre Company produced the musical *Quilters* at Lewis & Clark College. After the stage house was built, the proscenium hole was covered with plywood. The entire next season was performed in the old gym space, and the stage house was left vacant that whole time. The construction company spent the summer tearing out the seats and walls in the old space. Workers then built new walls and installed new seating. In summer 2003, Lakewood Theatre Company performed the musical *The Spitfire Grill* at Lewis & Clark College.

FRONT-ROW SEAT. The single chair shown here was representative of the front-row seats. The seating area provides good sight lines for every guest, and no seat is farther than 35 feet away from the stage. In fall 2003, Lakewood Theatre Company opened with *Joseph and the Amazing Technicolor Dreamcoat* in the newly completed Headlee Mainstage.

ORCHESTRA PIT. This is a lowered section in front of the stage that allows musicians to play. The curved concrete walls are designed to provide the best possible acoustics throughout the theater without overwhelming the stage performers. The general layout of the orchestra and the dimensions of the orchestra pit are essential. The conductor and musicians need to be able to see the performers to avoid missing cues. However, if the conductor sits too high, they could hit the pit ceiling with their stick.

THEATER WALLS. Kurt Herman is shown pointing to the newly constructed framing of the back wall of the seating area. A catwalk was constructed surrounding the seating area above and behind the last row of seats. It provides access to the lighting booth, and its railing is used for stage-lighting positions. Heating and cooling ducts are attached to the ceiling above this catwalk. A new ship's ladder was constructed to provide access to the lighting booth. During construction, Herman pulled the microphone and speaker wires through the finished conduit. Herman started running the light board for shows in 1994 for Larry Hutson, who was then the technical director. When Hutson left in 1997, Herman took over as technical director, and he remained in that role for 24 years. This image shows the lines of the old gym floor from when the building was a school.

ALL IN THE FAMILY. Kurt Herman comes from a theatrical family. His father, George Herman played Herbie in *Gypsy* in Honolulu; his stepmother Trisha DuBay played Nellie Forbush in *South Pacific* and appeared in numerous other plays; and his siblings Chris, Erik, and Lisa have all appeared on stage at Lake Oswego Community Theatre. In February 1980, this photograph was taken while the play *Candida* was being performed at the Honolulu Community Theatre before it became Diamond Head Theatre. This play was directed by George Herman, who had problems with cast members dropping out of this production because they got roles in either *Hawaii Five-0* or *Magnum, P.I.* So, George cast his relatives—Kurt as Lexy Mill, Chris as Eugene Marchbanks, and DuBay as Miss Proserpine Garnett. From left to right are Al Eben, Kurt Herman, and DuBay. (Courtesy of Diamond Head Theatre.)

THEATER ENTRANCE. In 2003, the workers pulled double shifts to put in decorative flooring, carpet, and acoustical materials. The design of this Marmoleum floor was created by Karol Niemi Associates. Each piece of the puzzle was cut by laser and placed without the use of adhesives. Above is a look at the box office window and the entryway into the theater in 2003. Below is another view of the entryway, where curated artworks are displayed. When new pieces arrive, the rotation of the art embodies a fresh look and contributes to regular visits by artists and enthusiasts.

REDESIGN OF ENTRYWAY. The entryway has been redesigned a few times. The 2012 redesign shown here included a fireplace, oversized marble tiles, and comfortable chairs with small tables. The gallery added a removable bar, a sink cabinet, a storage area, and portable tables and chairs. Two folding doors were added to the entry of the gallery space, along with space for an upright piano. The furniture was sturdy yet lightweight and could be moved quickly. In 2021, the latest redesign of the entryway was dedicated as the Dee Denton Gallery.

ILLUSTRATION OF THE 2012 REDESIGN. Phil Chek Residential and Commercial Design created this illustration for the 2012 redesign. Construction began on the entryway in July 2012 and was completed on September 30. This was part of the Phase I Capital Campaign in the $1.5 million renovation project that included the Artist Training Facility/rehearsal hall (later renamed Warner Hall), the sewer system, and remodeling of the office. Donations were collected from January 2012 through December 2018.

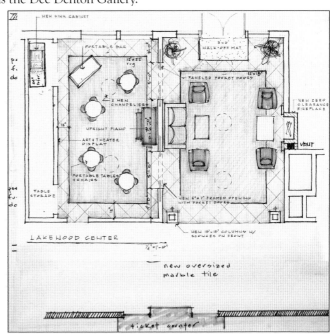

ARTIST TRAINING FACILITY. Overseeing the Artist Training Facility construction project were executive producer Kay Griffin Vega (left) and executive director Andrew Edwards (right). Both were essential in various aspects of the theater, guiding its programs, fundraising, and long-range planning. The Artist Training Facility was built with the exact same dimensions as the Headlee Mainstage. The performers no longer had to rehearse in classroom spaces that lacked adequate space for big dance numbers.

WARNER HALL DEDICATION. Below, supporters watch the Warner Hall dedication ceremony on September 18, 2015. The Artist Training Facility was renamed to honor arts and education advocates Bill and Barbara Warner. After the presentation, supporters were given the opportunity to take permanent markers and write "graffiti" on the panels inside Warner Hall. The Warners wrote: "All the World's a Stage—Babs & Bill."

YOUNG FRANKENSTEIN. "It's Alive!" The musical comedy *Young Frankenstein* was performed by Lakewood Theatre Company from September 12 through October 19, 2014. From left to right are Lisa Knox (as Frau Blücher), Burl Ross (as Igor), Evan Howells (as Dr. Frederick Frankenstein), and Danielle Valentine (as Inga). Ross kept the brain of Igor as a souvenir. *Young Frankenstein* is based on the 1974 film written by Mel Brooks and Gene Wilder. The story is set in 1930s Transylvania. Dr. Frankenstein inherits an estate from his deranged grandfather Victor Von Frankenstein. The grandfather's mad experiments that involved reanimating the dead continue under the guidance of Dr. Frederick Frankenstein with help from his servants Igor, Inga, and the fearsome Frau Blücher.

YOUNG FRANKENSTEIN CREW. As Frankenstein's monster is brought to life on stage, the crew backstage is providing its life's blood. In the 2014 Lakewood Community Theatre production of *Young Frankenstein*, manufacturing the hilarious and sometimes scary atmosphere took hard work from a creative team that included Michael Snider (director), Kay Griffin Vega (producer), Steve Knox (assistant to the director), and Cyndy Ramsey-Rier (musical director). Others on the crew included scenic designer Alan Schwanke, lighting designer Kurt Herman, stage manager Michael DeMaio, sound designer Marcus Storey, Patti Gosser, hair designer Jane Holmes, Felix Kelsey, and assistant stage manager Zach Peak. Pictured here are, from left to right: (first row, kneeling/sitting/squatting) Kris Bradford, DeMaio (seated on the throne), Tony Laundrie, and Mandy Wade; (second row, standing) Kerra Blakely, Kelsey, Storey, Herman, and Gosser; (in the background on the stairs) Hannah Gately, Peak, Joe Asselmeir, and Mychal Elmore. Snider noted that "every rehearsal was full of laughs, and I can attest to the devoted hard work of everyone involved."

Five

FESTIVAL OF THE ARTS

FIRST LAKE OSWEGO FESTIVAL OF THE ARTS. The Festival of the Arts was originally named the Arts & Flowers Festival, which was founded in 1963. It was created as a partnership between the Lake Oswego Art Guild and the Lake Oswego Chamber of Commerce. The festival moved to under the umbrella of the Lakewood Center for the Arts, a nonprofit arts center, in 1994. The festival is committed to arts education, performance, and exhibition. The Lake Oswego Festival of the Arts is an annual community-wide event that has been held at Lakewood Center for the Arts and George Rogers Park in modern times. (Courtesy of Lake Oswego Library.)

TACK THIS UP

1963

PERFORMING ARTS CALENDAR
FOR
LAKE OSWEGO
ANNUAL
ARTS & FLOWERS FESTIVAL

SAT. MAY 15
TO
MAY 25

THEATER
GREENWOOD
STATE ST
NO. SHORE
A. AVE

DATE	TIME	EVENT
SATURDAY MAY 15	10:00 AM	FESTIVAL PARADE-START GEORGE ROGERS PARK
	2:00 PM	CHILDREN'S STORY THEATRE
	4:00 PM	TEENAGE CONCERT - Jay Zilka "[Gentlemen Wild]"
SUNDAY MAY 16	4:00 PM	SUNDAY AFTERNOON JAZZ CONCERT
		PLUS
		RUTH MEYER, FOLK SINGER
	8:00 PM	SUNDAY EVENING CONCERT, Woodwind and Brass Ensembles - PORTLAND STATE MUSIC DEPARTMENT
MONDAY MAY 17	8:00 PM	POTPOURRI OF BROADWAY MUSICALS
		Lewis & Clark Theatre Department-Destry Rides Again
		Lake Oswego High School-Sound of Music
		Beaverton High School-Finian's Rainbow
TUESDAY MAY 18	8:00 PM	TRADITIONAL FOLK, SPANISH AND GYPSY AND CLASSICAL DANCE CONCERT-Ballet House-Portland
		ALSO
		THE CHANTELLES, Folk Singers, Marylhurst
WEDNESDAY MAY 19	8:00 PM	"THE TRICKERIES OF SCAPPINO" a play reading by THE ONE NIGHTERS
THURSDAY MAY 20	8:00 PM	A NIGHT WITH SHAKESPEARE-Excerpts from plays
FRIDAY MAY 21	8:00 PM	GLORIA CUTSFORTH, Soprano
SATURDAY MAY 22	2:00 PM	CHILDREN's STORY THEATRE
	4:00 PM	PUPPET SHOW-John Rausch and Page Long, Channel 10 TV Stars
	8:00 PM	CATHERINE CASSARNO's BALLET du LAC
		ALSO
		SELECTIONS FROM 110 IN THE SHADE-Lewis & Clark Tent Theatre

EXHIBITS

Lake Area Artists	Children & Adult	Children's Art
Old Safeway Store	Babb Building	432 1st Street
459 1st Street	Lake Grove	Lake Oswego
	Floral & Table Display	Long Alley Gallery
	Babb Building	358 State Street Alley
	Lake Grove	Lake Oswego

ALL PERFORMANCES FREE! AT L.O. COMMUNITY THEATRE

ARTS & FLOWERS FESTIVAL FIRST PROGRAM. This program of activities from the inaugural 1963 festival included floral art, ballet, jazz, antiques, white elephant sales, and a puppet show. The festival took place at various businesses, including Kingsbury's and Wizer's, art centers, Lewis & Clark College, Lake Oswego High School, Lakewood School, and Marylhurst University. (Courtesy of Lake Oswego Library.)

ARTS & FLOWERS FESTIVAL VOLUNTEERS. This is a photograph from an early Arts & Flowers Festival, which was the predecessor to the Lake Oswego Festival of the Arts. Identified in this image are Shirley Gladsby (as the minstrel at farthest left), June Kroft (at far right, in the picture frame), and Deanne Clinkscales (in the center, wearing a tuxedo). Planning for the festival is a year-round endeavor, and many committees work to fundraise, train, promote, and educate for what has become a major production. Today, it is sustained by valuable partnerships with the City of Lake Oswego, Clackamas County Tourism and Development Council, the Lake Oswego Chamber of Commerce, the Lake Oswego Rotary Club, the Lake Oswego School District, local businesses, and the Friends of the Festival, plus more than 500 volunteers who work throughout the year to make the festival a success. (Courtesy of Lake Oswego Library.)

CLACKAMAS COUNTY ASSOCIATED CHAMBER OF COMMERCE. Pictured on January 9, 1964, are, from left to right: (first row) Mrs. Chuck Olson, Dee Denton, and Jane Cik; (second row) Chuck Olson, James Martin, Bill Gilbert, Dee Thomason, Robert Robinson, and Aubrey Day. In 1963, Denton became executive director of the Lake Oswego Chamber of Commerce and quickly got started on a variety of initiatives to help grow chamber membership and the city. That same year, Mary Goodall and Marion Munger, founders of the Lake Oswego Art Guild, walked into Denton's office and suggested having a citywide arts festival. Denton thought it would be a great way to bring the community together, and so it began. The annual event proved also to be an economic success for local businesses. (Courtesy of Lake Oswego Library.)

OPEN ART SHOW. Since 1963, the Festival Open Art Show has welcomed visitors to view and purchase art, meet noted artists, and see demonstrations. Many and varied artists are encouraged to participate in the non-juried open show. When the Festival of the Arts increased in size, a pavilion tent was temporarily constructed outside Lakewood Center for the Arts. The festival occurs each June and attracts over 25,000 visitors every year. This photograph was taken on May 13, 1965. The painting is of a Colt revolver. From left to right are Joan Wing, Dorothy Schreiber, Dell Murphy, and Nancy Rowinski. (Courtesy of Lake Oswego Library.)

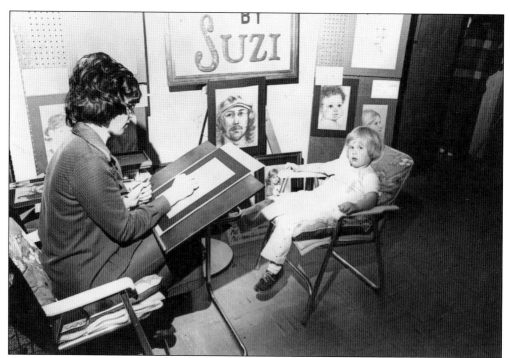

FESTIVAL AT LAKEWOOD SCHOOL, 1975. The 12th annual Lake Oswego Festival of the Arts was held at the Lakewood School from June 26 to June 29, 1975. Above, Suzi Collison, with her "Portraits by Suzi," demonstrated the art of oil painting. Over 500 original works of art were on display in the main exhibit hall in the gymnasium. Tents and booths were erected on the school playground for the arts and craft bazaar, where over 70 artists were on hand to discuss their works. This offered an opportunity for any artist, professional or amateur, of any age, to exhibit their work in almost any media. Below is a look at Lakewood's main corridor with art displayed on every wall; the classrooms featured a High School Senior Exhibit, a Showcase of Invited Artists, a Poster Gallery, and many more exhibits.

BICENTENNIAL FESTIVAL OF THE ARTS.
In 1976, the Festival of the Arts was held at Lakewood School. The exhibits were grouped by the idea of theme rather than by medium. There were seven principal bicentennial themes. Professional and nonprofessional work was separated. The themes were the Face and Figure of America (sculptures and portraits), Old Glory (colors red, white, and blue), From Sea to Shining Sea (seascapes), Thy Woods and Templed Hills (landscapes), Above the Fruited Plain (floral and fruit), Oh Beautiful for Spacious Skies (aviation and space), My Country 'Tis of Thee (regional representations), and The Hands of America (wood and metal works). Some of the live performances were offered by Lake Oswego Community Theatre (with free admission) and the Lilliput Players, with direction by Steve Knox.

Lake Oswego

Thirteenth Annual

FESTIVAL OF THE ARTS

1776! 1976!

Lakewood School-June 24,25,26,27

368 S. State Street — Lake Oswego, Oregon
Noon to 10 p.m., Sunday 'til 9 p.m.

Sponsored by the Lake Oswego Chamber of Commerce

THE LAKE OSWEGO CHAMBER OF COMMERCE
PROUDLY PRESENTS
THE THIRTEENTH ANNUAL FESTIVAL OF THE ARTS
June 24-25-26-27, 1976

CALENDAR OF ACTIVITIES & DEMONSTRATIONS

THURSDAY, JUNE 24
1-3 p.m.	Bonsai planting technique	Lee Hildebrand, Imperial Flowers
1-3 p.m.	Pottery - Bonsai trays	Carole McDonald
2:30-5 p.m.	Navajo weaving	Audrey Moore
2:30-5 p.m.	Spinning	Virginia Gallagher
3-5 p.m.	Frame-it-yourself	Heather Crisman
3:30-5 p.m.	Acrylic painting	Gen Stanley
8:30-9:15 p.m.	"Down in the Valley" by Kurt Weill	Lake Oswego Chamber Choir
	Lake Oswego Community Theater	Directed by Donald Riss
	156 Greenwood Rd. (No admission charge)	and Steve Knox

FRIDAY, JUNE 25
1-3 p.m.	Watercolor painting	Jean Schwalbe
1-3 p.m.	Creative art activities	Bernie Kluber and
	Painting & collage - For all ages - 25¢ charge	Aphra Katzer
2-4 p.m.	Watercolor portraits	Ken Carter
2-4 p.m.	Pastel portraits	Kaura Carter
3-4:30 p.m.	Needlepoint	Bill Cornet
3-5 p.m.	Palette knife painting	Millie Van Sickle
		Millie's Tiffany Shade Gallery
4-6 p.m.	Origami	Virginia Campbell
7 p.m.	Lilliput Players, family entertainment	Steve Knox, Director
8:30 p.m.	Opera & Ballet - selected works	Ballet du Lac and
	Lake Oswego Community Theater	Dorothy Fisher Jones
	156 Greenwood Rd. (No admission charge)	School of Opera & Related Arts

SATURDAY, JUNE 26
1-3 p.m.	Spinning & inkle weaving	Paul & Marie Schafer
		and Dorothy Scott - Clackamas Shuttle Guild
1-4 p.m.	Creative art activities	Bernie Kluber and
	Painting & collage - For all ages - 25¢ charge	Aphra Katzer
2-4 p.m.	Watercolor painting	Sue Hamilton
2-5 p.m.	Clown, puppets, & minstrels strolling the grounds	
2:30-5 p.m.	Cartography (historic map making)	Judith A. Farmer & John S. Phillips
		Northwest Cartographic Institute
3-4:30 p.m.	U-Frame It	Chris Kantor
		Classic Picture Framing
4-6 p.m.	Stained glass	Stuart Olson
4-6 p.m.	Sculpture - metal & plaster	Gary Berry
8 p.m.	"Dixieland" - Jazz at the Bank	Rose City Jazz Band
	Co-Sponsored by The Jazz Society of Oregon at the Oregon Bank.	
	Fourth & A Avenue - $3.00 admission	

SUNDAY, JUNE 27
1-3 p.m.	Bonsai planting technique	Lee Hildebrand, Imperial Flowers
1-3 p.m.	Pottery - Bonsai trays	Carole McDonald
1-4 p.m.	Creative art activities, Painting & collage	Bernie Kluber and
	For all ages - 25¢ charge	Aphra Katzer
2-5 p.m.	Clown, puppets, minstrels strolling the grounds	
4 p.m.	Concert	Lake Oswego Community Band
		Directed by Larry Hurst
4-6 p.m.	Oil portraits	Jean Davis

OPEN ART SHOW IN THE GYMNASIUM & CORRIDORS
Plants & interior arrangements by Gerber Gardens
ARTS & CRAFTS BAZAAR IN CLASSROOMS
"ONE-MAN" ART EXHIBITS
See list of sponsors for locations

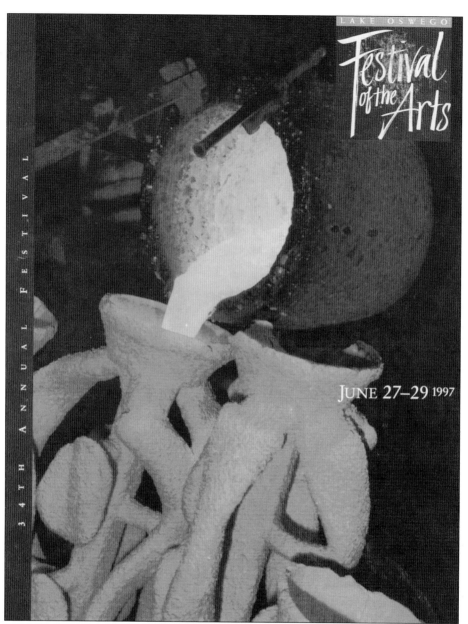

ANCIENT ART FORMS. The lost wax process of bronze sculpture was demonstrated at the 1997 Festival of the Arts. Arts education is a central part of the festival. Visitors can see firsthand how the lost was method of casting takes place. Bronze sculpture dates back almost 5,000 years, making it one of the oldest art forms still in use. The process of the lost wax method of bronze casting involves creating an image in clay. The work is cut into pieces, and a silicone rubber mold is applied, which creates a reverse impression of the work. Hot wax is poured into the mold and pulled out, leaving a hollow impression. A ceramic shell is molded around the wax castings. When the ceramic shell is heating, the wax melts away. Bronze is heated to 2,000 degrees or hotter and poured into the hollow space. When the mold is broken open, everything that was wax is now metal. The show offered demonstrations of various stages in the process and how freeing it can be to use this kind of medium.

LAKE OSWEGO FESTIVAL OF THE ARTS TURNS 50. On June 21, 22, and 23, 2013, the Festival of the Arts marked its 50th anniversary. Special thanks went to Dee Denton and the members of the Lake Oswego Chamber of Commerce, who had the vision to start the community-wide arts festival 50 years prior. More than 50 steering committee members worked together for a year to ensure that this event was extra special. Artists from previous festivals were invited to display both past and recent works. Pictured below are longtime advocates for the arts Joan Sappington (left) and her daughter Carrie O'Bryan. Sappington served as director of the festival for 15 years.

CRAFT FAIRE. The Craft Faire, now renamed Art in the Park, is a juried art exhibition. In 1997, the Craft Faire featured 75 artists and crafters and drew more than 200 applicants. In 2019, more than 300 artists applied, and of those, 120 were allowed to participate. The artwork must be handcrafted. In the 1997 festival program, Susan Noack, executive director of the festival, stated, "Jewelry is the most competitive category, but it showcases everything from natural stone fountains to children's fairytale costumes." (Author's collection.)

ART IN THE PARK. In 2021, the festival's Art in the Park coordinators and crew managed a record-breaking high temperature of 112 degrees at George Rogers Park by opening earlier in the morning. This table full of work by Palm Springs, California, artist Hong Rubenstein of One Dream Design includes a coronavirus (COVID-19) sculpture—one of the pieces reflective of the times. (Author's collection.)

Six

THE SHOW MUST GO ON

EMPTY HOUSE. In an industry that demands that "the show must go on," the novel coronavirus (COVID-19) has had a significant impact on Lakewood Center for the Arts. The last performance of *The Odd Couple* was held on March 15, 2020. The production run resumed in September 2021 after bans of public gatherings were lifted and new protocols were put into place. Exchanges, refunds, or donations of tickets were encouraged during this time. (Author's collection.)

STUDENTS RETURN TO LAKEWOOD. On June 29, 2020, campers were welcomed back to the Lakewood Center for the first time since its closing on March 16, 2020. In this image, Silas, age eight, is having his temperature checked by office manager Shelley Aisner before entering the building. The campers attended "Kids Create," taught by Liz Hayden. Camps were held in the theater's ballet studio, which is designed for easy awareness of social distancing. Camps had a 10-child limit in accordance with state mandates and safety regulations. Campers explored the building and had fun on the stage as well as playing outside and doing the usual hunts, games, and activities. Silas's mom, Melissa, a kindergarten teacher, said, "I wish they called it physical distancing instead of social distancing. Kids need to be social." (Author's collection.)

LAKEWOOD CENTER ASSOCIATES' SALE. New safety precautions were put into place for the Lakewood Center Associates' sale on October 14, 2020. At this annual event, donated items such as antiques, jewelry, and furniture are resold to the public, and the proceeds are donated to the Lakewood Center for the Arts for renovations and improvements. (Author's collection.)

MASKS HANDMADE BY VOLUNTEERS. Volunteer stitchers made over 100 masks from discarded fabric and old costumes to distribute to the local community when supplies were extremely limited and mask mandates were on the horizon. This mask was made by Jessica Carr Miller, and the fabric was from a production of *Nine*, the musical.

CLEANING OUT THE PROP SHOP. Volunteers Kay Olsen (left), Dick Spence (right), and Leanne Spence (not shown) visited weekly for six weeks during 2021 to help with the cleanup of the Lakewood Theatre Company's prop shop. The volunteers sorted props from *Monty Python's Spamalot*, *Man of La Mancha*, and other plays. Props that were no longer useful were donated to other theaters, schools, or local nonprofits. (Author's collection.)

SMOKY SKIES. During the summer of 2020, when indoor performances were put on hold due to COVID-19, another challenge came to the forefront in the form of one million acres that burned in the state of Oregon. The smoke-filled skies and poor air quality led to the postponement of Lakewood's outdoor concert series. Many homes and businesses in the area were without power. Lakewood staff members and others helped with evacuation efforts. (Author's collection.)

LAKEWOOD ON THE LAWN. Outdoor concerts were briefly put on hold until the air quality improved. This socially distanced crowd (and the dog) are enjoying the sounds of 3 Leg Torso on the lawn in front of the center. Béla Balogh is a former Lakewood student who took a peek inside his former classroom, which is now a ballet studio. Balogh and his band, 3 Leg Torso, performed at the Lakewood on the Lawn concert series in 2020. Balogh plays the violin, Courtney Von Drehle plays the accordion, Bill Athens plays bass, and T.J. Arko plays percussion. (Author's collection.)

ONLINE CLASSES. After a brief shutdown, some classes, such as "Starstruck: TV/film acting," ballet, "Zooming with Shakespeare," and "Pocket Sketching" were offered online. Other camps and classes welcomed small groups back into the classrooms and outdoor areas. Classes were limited in size and held in accordance with all state mandates and safety regulations. (Author's collection.)

ONLINE PERFORMANCES. Burl Ross, a Lakewood Theatre Company actor since 1970, performed online during quarantine with his fun-packed retelling of stories from the past. Many props and memorabilia were collected, including Igor's brain from *Young Frankenstein*, the sword from *Three Musketeers* (in which he played the King of France), and the exaggerated manhood created for *The Scandalous Adventures of Sir Toby Trollope*. Ross also reunited with former Lilliput Players Steve and Lisa Knox (below) for some comedy gold. Lilliput Players was a performing and touring children's theater troupe that used Lakewood Theatre Company as their home location during the 1970s. (Both, author's collection.)

Welcome Back, Spence and Camp. Dick and Leanne Spence graciously volunteered their time to usher during the last performance of *The Odd Couple* on March 15, 2020, prior to the closing of the theater, and again for the first performance of the reopening night on September 23, 2021. The first patrons through the door were Lakewood Theatre Company supporters Fritz and Barbara Camp. Pictured here are, from left to right, Dick, Leanne, Fritz, and Barbara. The Dee Denton Gallery is visible in the background. (Author's collection.)

First Crowd for the Reopening of *The Odd Couple*. An enthusiastic crowd from The Springs Living retirement center gathered for the final dress rehearsal night before the reopening for *The Odd Couple*. About 45 people attended the reopening on September 23, 2021. (Author's collection.)

RIBBON-CUTTING CEREMONY FOR THE DEE DENTON GALLERY. On June 25, 2021, the newly renovated Lakewood Center Entryway Gallery was dedicated as the Dee Denton Gallery. The Denton family held a private dedication ceremony and introduced the first exhibit in the gallery: Dee Denton's personal art collection. Lake Oswego mayor Joe Buck is shown speaking about Dee Denton's legacy. (Author's collection.)

GOV. KATE BROWN CONGRATULATES LAKEWOOD THEATRE COMPANY. The governor of Oregon, Kate Brown, congratulated Lakewood Theatre Company on its 70th anniversary in 2022. As Oregon's 38th governor, she worked closely with the Oregon Health Authority to implement vaccine rollouts and safety measures during the COVID-19 pandemic. (Courtesy of the Oregon Governor's Office.)

DISCOVER THOUSANDS OF LOCAL HISTORY BOOKS
FEATURING MILLIONS OF VINTAGE IMAGES

Arcadia Publishing, the leading local history publisher in the United States, is committed to making history accessible and meaningful through publishing books that celebrate and preserve the heritage of America's people and places.

Find more books like this at
www.arcadiapublishing.com

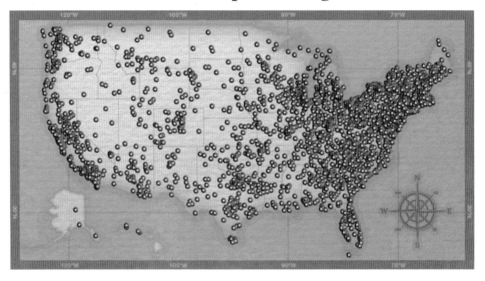

Search for your hometown history, your old stomping grounds, and even your favorite sports team.

Consistent with our mission to preserve history on a local level, this book was printed in South Carolina on American-made paper and manufactured entirely in the United States. Products carrying the accredited Forest Stewardship Council (FSC) label are printed on 100 percent FSC-certified paper.

MADE IN THE USA